# AESCHYLUS

# THE ORESTEIAN TRILOGY

## AGAMEMNON · THE CHOEPHORI
## THE EUMENIDES

✻

TRANSLATED BY
## PHILIP VELLACOTT

## PENGUIN BOOKS

## PENGUIN BOOKS

Published by the Penguin Group
Penguin Books Ltd, 80 Strand, London WC2R 0RL, England
Penguin Putnam Inc., 375 Hudson Street, New York, New York 10014, USA
Penguin Books Australia Ltd, 250 Camberwell Road, Camberwell, Victoria 3124, Australia
Penguin Books Canada Ltd, 10 Alcorn Avenue, Toronto, Ontario, Canada M4V 3B2
Penguin Books India (P) Ltd, 11 Community Centre, Panchsheel Park, New Delhi – 110 017, India
Penguin Books (NZ) Ltd, Cnr Rosedale and Airborne Roads, Albany, Auckland, New Zealand
Penguin Books (South Africa) (Pty) Ltd, 24 Sturdee Avenue, Rosebank 2196, South Africa

Penguin Books Ltd, Registered Offices: 80 Strand, London WC2R 0RL, England

www.penguin.com

This translation published 1956
Reprinted with revisions 1959
046

Copyright © Philip Vellacott, 1956, 1959
All rights reserved

Printed in England by Clays Ltd, St Ives plc
Set in Monotype Perpetua

*The terms for performance of these plays may
be obtained from the League of Dramatists,
84 Drayton Gardens, London SW10 9RD,
to whom all applications for
permission should
be made*

ISBN-13: 978-0-14-044067-6

www.greenpenguin.co.uk

# CONTENTS

This translation of the *Oresteia* was commissioned by the British Broadcasting Corporation, and was first broadcast in the Third Programme on Sunday, 27 May 1956, with the following cast:

| | |
|---|---|
| Clytemnestra | Margaret Rawlings |
| Orestes | Peter Wyngarde |
| Agamemnon | Howard Marion-Crawford |
| Cassandra | Beth Boyd |
| Aegisthus | Malcolm Hayes |
| A Watchman | Cyril Shaps |
| A Herald | Denis McCarthy |
| Electra | Nicolette Bernard |
| A Servant | Cecil Bellamy |
| A Nurse | Nan Marriott-Watson |
| The Pythian Priestess | Gladys Young |
| Apollo | Deryck Guyler |
| Athene | Joan Hart |

The Choruses were spoken by

Leon Quartermaine
with

*Agamemnon* { Carleton Hobbs
Francis de Wolff
Godfrey Kenton

*Choephori* { Dorothy Holmes-Gore
Mary Law
Susan Richards

*Eumenides* { Denys Blakelock
Denis Goacher
John Gabriel
Howieson Culff
Kelty MacLeod
Molly Lumley

The Choruses were sung by

Stephen Manton
Mary Rowland
and
The Ambrosian Singers

The Music was composed by Antony Hopkins. The Boyd Neel Orchestra (led by Joshua Glazier) was conducted by the composer

The plays were produced for radio by Raymond Raikes

# INTRODUCTION

A PROPER introduction to these plays, even for the reader who knows no Greek, would occupy a whole volume much larger than this little book. Their subject-matter is so near to the core of human feeling, to the central experiences of life from which all human studies take their origin, that the careful reader of them finds himself turning aside, now to history and pre-history, now to philosophy, theology, and ethics, now to the development of drama as an art; and all the time held by the intensity of the author's poetic conception which springs to life in line after line like an inexhaustible fountain. In the following pages I shall not attempt even to summarize the wealth of learned, imaginative, and critical writing which is available in libraries for the enrichment of our understanding of this work; but merely to give the minimum of information necessary for a first reading. Those who already have some knowledge, even if slight, of the world in which Aeschylus lived will find their desire for further reading best satisfied by selecting from the short list of books given on page 197.

In modern times the Oresteian trilogy has rightly been accorded a place among the greatest achievements of the human mind. Much of the dramatic excitement, much of the philosophic intensity, of this work, perhaps also some hint of its poetic splendour, may reach the modern reader through a translation. But the basis of it all is a story which, like many great stories, grew gradually into shape through several centuries; a story compounded of fact and imagination, reflecting the experience, belief, and aspiration of a vital society, and blending within itself the poetry of common life and the vision of the prophet. It is a long story, and has been told very often. In telling it once more, for the interest of those who read the plays for the first time, I must begin with the remotest myth, and end with documented history.

In the beginning of the world, Ouranos was king of the gods. He was the sky, and Gaia, the earth, was his wife. Of the age during which he reigned very little is known. Certain other deities were already established in power, notably Fate, or Moira. In time Ouranos and his age declined and disappeared, and Cronos his son reigned in his stead.

During the reign of Cronos the human race was created. The number of deities increased, and their functions became more distinct. Man was kept in a state of wretched weakness and subservience; but our race from its first appearance proved a source of irresistible fascination to the immortals. They tried to impose on man certain principles of behaviour; and man in turn tried various ingenious ways of influencing gods and the powers of nature to favour his enterprises. The age of Cronos was in general characterized as the age of anarchy, the time before the institution of property, the establishment of cities, or the framing of laws. We may fairly infer that it was not gods, but humans, who first began to be dissatisfied with the blessings of anarchy; and one god was on their side, Prometheus, a son of the earth, himself the germ of intelligence in a brute universe, the germ of moral order in the midst of blank confusion. Nature itself was similarly dissatisfied, and stirring towards the principle of order. The time ripened for a new dynasty.

So, some time in the third millennium B.C. (a date may establish some relation between myth and history), there occurred that strange and unquestionable event which was the vision Keats realized in 'Hyperion'. From the sea and the mountains, from forest and stream, young gods and goddesses were born, whose eyes expressed knowledge and imagination, laughter and feeling, order and control. Their chief was Zeus, whose name, which means the sky, claimed direct descent from Ouranos. The old order rallied its forces against the new; but Prometheus belonged by nature to the age of reason and law, and by his help the cosmic battle was won, the age of anarchy defeated, and the Olympian dynasty established.

Prometheus was rewarded for his services with an invitation to dine at the table of the Olympian gods. There, in pity for the sad plight of mankind, he stole a spark of divine fire and conveyed it to the earth. He taught men all the uses of fire, and in particular how to melt metal and shape it into weapons and tools. Zeus, seeing what increase of strength and confidence men would gain from fire, was angry that divine supremacy should be so imperilled, and demanded repentance and complete submission from Prometheus. When the champion of mankind proved defiant, Zeus sent Hephaestus, the Olympian fire-god, to chain him to a rocky peak in the Caucasus mountains. This event forms the opening scene of Aeschylus' play, *Prometheus Bound*.

Prometheus continued his defiance of tyranny, and reinforced it by declaring that he knew an ancient prophecy, revealed to him by his mother, the earth (the original holder of all foreknowledge), which threatened the ultimate downfall of Zeus unless he should be warned in time. For a thousand years Prometheus endured the successive torments which Zeus inflicted to make him reveal the prophecy; until at last Zeus turned from violence to reason and offered Prometheus release and pardon in return for his secret. This stage in the story brings us to about the middle of the second millennium B.C.

Prometheus then revealed the prophecy. It concerned one of the sea-nymphs named Thetis, whose destiny was 'to bear a son greater than his father'. Zeus had relented only just in time; he was already enamoured of this nymph and contemplating a union. Prometheus was released, and Zeus immediately chose a mortal husband for Thetis, a young man named Peleus who had sailed with Jason in the ship *Argo*. Such delighted interest had been aroused among the Olympian deities by this dénouement, that they consented to attend the wedding-feast in a body.

All the gods were invited, except (naturally) a minor power called Eris, the goddess of strife. Eris, however, came uninvited, and threw on to the table a golden apple inscribed 'For the fairest'. Hera, the wife of Zeus, Athene, the maiden goddess of wisdom and valour, and Aphrodite, the goddess of love, quarrelled for possession of the apple. To settle the matter, Zeus sent them to the most beautiful of mortal youths, Paris, the son of Priam king of Troy. Each goddess offered Paris a bribe: Hera offered supremacy in government, Athene supremacy in war; Aphrodite offered him the most beautiful of women for his wife. Paris gave the apple to Aphrodite.

Troy was a rich and powerful fortified city on the eastern side of the Dardanelles. (This modern name is derived from Dardanus, the founder of the Trojan race, who in Homer are called Dardanidae. The name 'Greeks', like the name 'Trojans', is a Latin word; Greece was 'Hellas', and its people 'Hellenes'.) The Trojan way of life had many features in common with that of the Greeks. Behaviour on the battlefield observed (or failed to observe) roughly the same conventions. Both nations were highly skilled in the training and use of horses. Both recognized as the unit of government a city in which an absolute and hereditary monarch ruled over citizens and the country people of the surrounding district. Both accepted slavery as an institution. But Greeks affected to regard Trojans as typical Orientals, as effeminate and irrational, as slavish subjects of despotic kings, as cruel, primitive, and unreliable. Greek tragedy, which was all written within a few generations of the final overthrow of monarchy in Athens, naturally expresses this contempt for despotism more strongly than Homer, who wrote when Greek cities were always ruled by kings; though it is probable that Greek kings took more notice of advice from their nobles than was customary further east.

One of the most powerful Greek cities in the second millennium B.C. was Argos, in the Peloponnese. Two brothers, Atreus and Thyestes, descended through Pelops from Tantalus (who, like Prometheus, feasted with gods and was punished for betraying their secrets), had quarrelled about succession to the throne of Argos; moreover, Thyestes had seduced Atreus' wife. Atreus reckoned that the score would be settled once for all if he could trick Thyestes into committing some unclean or sacrilegious act which would render him permanently taboo in the eyes of the Argive citizens. He secretly murdered Thyestes' two young sons, and served their flesh to Thyestes at a banquet. Thyestes went into exile and died there; but he had a third son, an infant called Aegisthus, whom he took with him and brought up in exile.

Atreus himself got away with murder; but such debts are not forgotten. His eldest son, Agamemnon, inherited the throne of Argos, and with it the curse that had settled on the family. His brother Menelaus later became king of Sparta in succession to his father-in-law Tyndareos. In the plays of Euripides we find Menelaus generally presented as an unpleasant character; but in the Oresteia (though he does not appear) he seems to command the love and loyalty of Argive citizens almost equally with Agamemnon.

Menelaus as a young man had been one among a great number of noble Greeks who had haunted the palace of Tyndareos king of Sparta. Tyndareos' wife Leda had been loved by Zeus, who visited her in the form of a swan. Leda bore Zeus twin daughters, Helen and Clytemnestra. (Both are often called 'daughter of Tyndareos'; but whereas Helen is as often called 'daughter of Zeus', Clytemnestra's divine parentage is seldom referred to.) Helen's extraordinary beauty attracted innumerable suitors and aroused such emotion that they all entered into a mutual pact: each man swore that he would accept Helen's choice as final, and offer his armed service to the husband, should his possession of her ever be threatened. By what principle, instinct or calculation Helen was led to choose Menelaus will remain one of the delightful puzzles of history. He was a good fighter; a man of few words and little wit. Almost the only other thing known about him is that he had auburn hair.

Agamemnon's character is clearer. He was 'every inch a king'; and he would have liked to be a thorough-going tyrant, but in general recognized the necessity for compromise with inferiors. His resentment at having to compromise was shown in a readiness to deceive on occasion; and itself arose from a deep-rooted weakness of will, and lack of confidence in his own authority. It was Agamemnon's inevitable fate to marry Helen's sister, Clytemnestra.

Clytemnestra is the most powerful figure in the *Oresteia*; one of the most powerful, indeed, in all dramatic literature; but this figure is very largely the imaginative creation of Aeschylus. Other writers of his period, whose works are lost to us, may have contributed something; but Homer gives only a meagre statement of the one act for which she was universally known, that she plotted with her lover to murder her husband. He neither examines her motives nor describes her character. When, however, we meet Clytemnestra in the *Oresteia*, we find her as vivid and fully developed a personality as the great heroes of the *Iliad*. She is the only character who appears in all three plays. Clearly Aeschylus intends her part in the drama to be significant. We must defer consideration of this until later, and meanwhile continue the story.

King Priam of Troy sent his youngest son, Paris, as ambassador to Sparta; there he was entertained by Clytemnestra's sister Helen. Menelaus, with what seems to have been his normal stupidity, found it necessary to sail to Crete on State business and leave Helen and Paris alone. Aphrodite fulfilled her promise. When Menelaus returned, he called upon all those who had been his fellow-suitors to fulfil theirs, and aid him in pursuing Helen to Troy, and burning to the ground that stronghold of Oriental lust and treachery. There was an almost universal response to his appeal, and Agamemnon was made Commander-in-Chief of a vast army and fleet which assembled at Aulis, a bay sheltered by the island of Euboea on the east coast of Greece.

When everything was ready for the start, the wind changed to the north. The usual fair-wind sacrifices failed to have their effect. Days lengthened into months, and still northerly gales kept the fleet harbour-bound, till food-supplies became an acute problem. At length the prophet Calchas pronounced that the anger of the virgin goddess Artemis must be appeased by the sacrifice of Agamemnon's virgin daughter Iphigenia. Agamemnon protested, and was taunted by his fellow-kings with faint-heartedness. In the end he wrote to Clytemnestra saying he had arranged for his daughter to be married to Achilles, and commanding her to be sent to Aulis. Iphigenia came, and was duly slaughtered. The wind veered, and the fleet set sail. In the ninth year of the siege Paris was killed in battle. In the tenth Troy was captured by the ruse of the wooden horse; all adult males were killed, the women and children enslaved, and the city reduced to ashes.

The play *Agamemnon* opens in Argos a few hours after the capture of Troy; and its climax is the murder of Agamemnon, on his return, by Clytemnestra. In *The Choephori* Agamemnon's son Orestes, who had grown up in exile, returns to Argos at Apollo's command to avenge his father; he kills both Clytemnestra and her lover Aegisthus, and departs pursued by the Furies. Finally, in *The Eumenides*, Orestes stands his trial before Athene and the Athenian court of Areopagus. The Furies accuse him, Apollo defends him; the mortal votes are evenly divided; and Athene gives her casting vote for his acquittal. The Furies at first threaten Athens with plagues, but are at last persuaded by Athene to accept a home and a position of honour in her city. Such is the bare outline of the three plays, which will be discussed in more detail later; but first it is necessary to give some brief account of the history and the ideas which form the background of the trilogy.*

In the 800 years between the fall of Troy and the rise of Athens, Greek social and political life underwent many changes. Each city and island for the most part maintained its independence; sometimes one city or group of cities was more powerful, sometimes another. Periods of prosperity and peace, by reducing the necessity for a unified command in the hands of a king, gradually transferred power from the kings to the nobles, then from the nobles to rich merchants who had risen by trade from the ranks of the peasants. By the seventh and sixth centuries merchants of outstanding ability or good luck established themselves in many cities as tyrants; and these tyrants tended to pay tribute to the powerful empire of Persia, which in return would guarantee their position. Finally, about the end of the sixth century a great movement for freedom resulted in the expulsion of most of the Greek tyrants and the establishment of democratic constitutions. The last tyrant of Athens was expelled in 510 B.C. He was with the Persian expedition which in 490 B.C. was utterly defeated by the Athenians at Marathon.

The plays of Aeschylus were all written within some thirty years after the battle of Marathon, while the new Athenian democracy was bursting into full life, and preparing with boundless confidence to take upon itself the leadership of the Greek world. Aeschylus and his contemporaries had spent their youth amidst tyrannies, revolutions, and wars. They were now called upon to govern, to judge, and to legislate. The new moral responsibility of the ordinary citizen was fully accepted and deeply felt. No important burden was delegated either to aristocrats or to officials; the citizens themselves decided in person, by a majority vote, all judicial and political questions. One problem, therefore, occupied their minds insistently: What is justice? What is the relation of justice to vengeance? Can justice be reconciled with the demands of religion, the force of human feeling, the intractability of Fate?

This problem was complicated for the contemporaries of Aeschylus

* For much of the material comprised in the following pages I am indebted to several valuable articles by Professor R. P. Winnington-Ingram, especially two contained in the *Journal of Hellenic Studies*, volumes LXVIII and LXXIV.

by the fact that religion spoke with a divided voice. There were indeed two religions inextricably mixed: the old religion and the new. The old religion, deriving from the period before the advent of Zeus and the Olympians, was in origin probably a worship of the dead, and therefore was concerned with placating the powers that live under the earth, the 'chthonian gods' (from *chthon*, the earth). The earth itself has, naturally, always been thought of as female, and other female deities were worshipped as well, such as the Fates and the Furies, and Themis, goddess of justice and order, the mother of Prometheus, whom Aeschylus identifies with Earth. The religious rites of the Eleusinian mysteries were also connected with this older religion, for they centred round the worship of Demeter, goddess of crops (the name means 'mother earth'), and her daughter Persephone, who was queen of the lower world. The Eleusinian rites, however, were mainly joyful in character, while the worship of chthonian powers was more generally associated with fear and mourning. The worship of the Olympians, on the other hand, was always an occasion of enjoyment; and dancing, athletic and dramatic performances, and feasting, were its natural modes of expression.

Legend described the rise of the new religion in terms of a 'theomachy', or battle of gods, in which Zeus and the Olympians overcame Cronos and the gods of the earth. History connects it with the invasion of Greece, some time in the fifteenth century B.C., by a warlike race from the north of Europe who called themselves Achaeans, and whose gods were closely related to the Nordic gods who figure in early English legend. These armed and organized invaders easily conquered the indigenous tribes, built themselves walled cities, and established dynasties, laws, and military traditions. The old order was not simply abolished; many of its cults and customs remained, and some of the older deities were still universally honoured. So by a whole series of expedient compromises the two religions flourished side by side, their opposite characters giving scope for a wide variety of personal preference in religious practice. It seems probable, however, that essential differences between the two religions from time to time made themselves strongly felt; and in the middle of the sixth century Pisistratus, 'tyrant' of Athens, did his best to strengthen the Olympian cults by the building of temples, by the establishment of the Panathenaic Festival (of which more will be said in connexion with *The Eumenides*), and by encouraging the circulation and public recitation of the Homeric poems. None the less, the old cults remained vital and popular, and their rivalry with the official religion was still keenly felt in the time of Aeschylus. The question of the relation of justice to vengeance was also the question of the relation of Zeus to the chthonian gods.

Pre-Olympian religion would roughly equate justice with vengeance; and the Furies were there to see that vengeance was exacted, whether by human or divine action. The function of the Furies was to punish three major sins: blasphemy against the gods, treachery to a host or guest, and the shedding of kindred blood. From very early times these sins were felt to threaten the basis of human society, and therefore to bring a curse on the community which condoned them. Thus the Furies, in hounding such sinners away from their homes, performed an essential and universal service; and for this they were honoured as Eumenides, or Kindly Ones; though the name certainly represented a desire to appease as well as a desire to honour. Their horrible aspect and relentless cruelty became the safeguard of cities. But Aeschylus shows clearly that their principles are inconsistent and unsatisfactory; for while they will punish a son who does not avenge his father, and punish equally a son who kills his mother, they will ignore the guilt of a wife who kills her husband, because he is not her blood-relation. This is an intolerable position; as Apollo points out, it implies a contempt for the marriage-bond; it also shows that the Furies act only by blind rule-of-thumb, and are incapable of dealing properly with a special case like that of Orestes. More than this, as far as the Furies are concerned, a single murder may lead to an insoluble feud and an endless series of murders in successive generations. In larger terms, then, the old religion is no safe moral guide in urgent situations which involve life and death; the quest for justice receives no solution from the chthonian gods.

The next source from which a reliable moral sanction may be sought is Apollo, who speaks through his oracle at Delphi. For many hundreds of years, since before the advent of Zeus, cities and individuals from every part of Greece, when faced with perpelxing problems, moral or political, had commonly sent to consult this oracle;

and the college of priests who administered it had acquired a unique position of influence in the whole Greek world, so that in any quarrel between States the support of Delphi might prove decisive. Just as the Hebrew law of the Old Testament, 'An eye for an eye and a tooth for a tooth', imposed an exact limit on the indiscriminate vengeance of primitive savagery, so the Delphic code enjoined the taking of life for life by the next of kin to a murdered man, and then offered to purify the avenger by ritual cleansing, and so avoid further murders and an endless feud. But this principle, though preferable to the blind and unlimited operation of the Furies, is still unsatisfactory. Acting on it, Apollo has instructed Orestes to kill his mother; an act which Orestes himself abhors as deeply as everyone who hears of it, as an offence against the tenderest of all natural affections. Apollo's code in this instance proves barbaric; and the barbaric basis of it is made very clear by Apollo himself when, in the opening scene of *The Eumenides*, he abuses those repellent beings whom he had himself used (see *Choeph.*, p. 113) as a threat to compel Orestes to carry out his command. Aeschylus shows that the quest for justice can hope for no final solution from Apollo and the principle of vengeance. (See further pp. 34–5.)

As *Agamemnon* is dominated by the relentlessness of Fate, *The Choephori* by the command of Apollo, so *The Eumenides* presents the true justice of Athene, expressed in the authority and wisdom of an established court of law, the Athenian Areopagus. In bringing on to the stage this ancient Athenian institution, as a body founded by Athene herself for the purpose of trying Orestes on a charge of murder, Aeschylus achieves two ends. First, as an ultimate solution of the deepest moral problems, he holds up something which we might describe as embodying the 'Athenian way of life', in contrast to the primitive ideas of the old religion and the inadequate compromise of the 'Delphic code'. But at the same time he deals with a burning political question of the day.

For the last 130 years, since the Constitution of Solon (about 592 B.C.), the Areopagus (so called because it met on the 'Hill of Ares') had held a dominating position in the political life of Athens. Its powers over every aspect of community life were considerable; and as its members were life-members, its practice tended to become reactionary. Within a generation after the battle of Marathon the progressive democracy of the Athenian Assembly had decided to shake off this curb of freedom. In 462 B.C., four years before the production of the *Oresteia*, the Areopagus had been deprived of all its powers except that of jurisdiction in cases of homicide. This revolutionary change had aroused intense feeling among both supporters and opponents. The position of the court of Areopagus was guarded by strong religious sanctions. The Eumenides, whose function was closely connected with the judicial powers of this court, had an immemorial shrine in a cavern at the foot of the same hill, and thus represented the guardianship of the chthonian gods. The Areopagites were recruited from the most wealthy Athenian classes. Thus the propertied aristocracy found themselves allied with the old-fashioned country folk in indignation at the radical dispossessing of their 'House of Lords'. A democratic leader named Ephialtes framed the resolution and carried the reform; he was murdered not long afterwards, and his murderer was never discovered.

It is to the tension caused by this dispute that Aeschylus addresses himself in the second half of *The Eumenides*. He asserts that the Areopagus from its foundation was not a political executive, but a judicial court. He states its divine sanctions in the highest possible terms; and by showing the Eumenides as yielding ultimately to Athene's patient persuasion, and accepting both the equal judgement of the Areopagites and Athene's casting vote, he pleads for a reasonable spirit of accommodation. When at the end of the play agreement is at last reached, those present on the stage are joined by a number of men and women of all ages, and children, who form a procession immediately recognizable as the great Panathenaic procession, the culminating event of the four-yearly Panathenaic Festival. A further link between past and present is found in the fact that one feature of the Panathenaic procession was a numerous contingent of the 'resident aliens' who had found a home in Athens; and now the Eumenides are welcomed by the name of 'resident aliens' – an honourable name, for Athenians prided themselves on the liberal welcome they extended to immigrants from other cities. Thus the grand drama of justice is made to end in the glorification of Athens and her supreme judicial court, in the reconciliation of the old order with the new, of

tradition with progress, of Fate with Zeus. And this final mention of
Zeus as lord of the new dispensation inaugurated by Athene is made
in such a way as to remind us that at various points throughout the
whole trilogy the name of Zeus has been associated also with the
earliest phase of man's development towards a proper understanding
of justice; with the unbending primitive law, 'The doer must suffer',
as well as with the sympathetic wisdom of Athene. The Furies, who
derived their authority from Fate, yet were from the beginning the
instruments of Zeus, have changed to the Eumenides, the Kindly Ones,
and now take their place as embodying that ultimate sanction of fear
which underlies the new order, as it dominated the old.

There is a second great question which Aeschylus considers in the
*Oresteia*; and it concerns the central figure of Clytemnestra. She is
first mentioned, by the Watchman, as a woman with a man's will. In
her first scene with the Elders, when she has ended her speech with
'These are a woman's words', they reply, 'Madam, your words are
like a man's.' Clytemnestra was right about the message of the
beacons, and the Elders were wrong. When the Herald arrives, she
shocks them into subservience by the boldness of her lying. Con-
fronted with her proud, forbidding husband, who with crushing sour-
ness tells her not to make a woman of him, she takes the man's part
and imposes her will. Once in the play she is defeated: she cannot
wrest a word from Cassandra. When the murder is done, she rails at
the Elders, whose unmanly indecision had paltered while the king
died, for still treating her as a thoughtless woman; and speaks of the
man she has chosen for her shield, Aegisthus – who is called 'woman'
by the Elders, and by Orestes in the next play. Her status as a wife
has been touched by both Chryseis and Cassandra – but that, though
galling enough, is of minor importance, since convention allowed a
soldier his concubine. Clytemnestra's tragedy both began and ended
with outrage to her motherhood, when Iphigenia was taken from
her, and when Orestes killed her. In the climax of *The Eumenides*, the
trial-scene, we have a long argument between Apollo and the Furies
on the respective rights and status of a man and a woman in marriage
and parenthood*; and a brief but emphatic argument on the rival

* This argument has sometimes been otherwise interpreted. For a full dis-
cussion of Athenian social history from the second millennium B.C., and the

claims to freedom of a husband and a wife finds a place also at the climactic moment of *The Choephori*, just before Orestes kills his mother. Clearly the relation of man and woman in marriage must be named, after the 'quest for justice', as the second great theme of the trilogy. The question remains, in what form was this matter felt as a living issue in Aeschylus' day?

Athenian society in that period gave to women a somewhat equivocal status, of which a good description is to be found in Professor Kitto's *The Greeks* (Penguin Books), pp. 219–36, though he perhaps over-estimates the happiness that women derived from their privileges. Since Aeschylus was born the personal liberty and social and political responsibility of every male citizen had increased immeasurably; and in this exhilarating expansion women had had very little share. Yet the personal qualities which in men produced the greatness of Athens must certainly have been present in women, and, denied proper expression, can only have engendered the poison of resentment and perverted ambition. A generation after Aeschylus, Euripides spoke explicitly for women in the person of Medea, who, like Clytemnestra, satisfied her indignation by murder. There were Clytemnestras in Athenian society in the fifth century, and a study of extant law-court speeches might suggest some names. Aeschylus does not justify his murderess, any more than Euripides justifies his Medea or Ibsen his Hedda Gabler; but he reiterates the dangerous anomalies which must occur when, in a social framework giving every freedom to men and none to women, a passionate and strong-willed wife confronts a weak but arrogant husband. Many Athenian marriages doubtless were based on love and some degree of personal equality, and gave scope to the wife to use her gifts and intelligence; but a woman whose marriage was less fortunate had neither redress nor escape, imprisoned in a position which denied her a due measure of freedom and respect. Athene in *The Eumenides* gives her vote to Orestes because 'in all things she is on the father's side'; that is to say, Athenian society is, and must be, a man-governed society. In such a society men are responsible for the position they impose upon women. Clytemnestra, then, is not merely a murderess, the horrifying instrument of pitiless

development from matriarchy through feudalism to tyranny and democracy, see Professor G. Thomson's *Aeschylus and Athens*.

justice. She is also the mother of Iphigenia, and, in that character, 'a symbol of all wives and mothers who suffer from the inferior status of the woman in marriage' (Winnington-Ingram).* She is driven to her murderous act not only by love of Aegisthus, hatred of Agamemnon, jealousy of Cassandra; the deepest spring of her tragedy is the knowledge that she, who has it in her to be the head of a kingdom, if need be, as well as of a family, can be freely ignored as a wife and outraged as a mother by a man she knows her inferior. She thus confronts the Athenians with a problem which it is evident they have not solved.

The other problem, however, the quest for justice in the relation of citizen with citizen, is, if not completely solved, at least shown to be within reach of solution through the wisdom of Athene as expressed in the democratic constitution which Aeschylus' fellow-citizens had evolved. Aeschylus had some reason for feeling that in the democracy of his day the political and social feuds and struggles of centuries, all conducted in the name of justice on one side at least, and often on both, had at last achieved their end; that the Athenian State offered a hopeful approach to every moral problem of society. His treatment of the theme of feud and reconciliation in the *Oresteia* suggests that he saw the same principle at work in history. He expresses it in two statements, which recur in various forms: *The doer must suffer*, and *By suffering man learns*. These are laws of Fate, and even Zeus must obey them. Zeus learnt in time to compromise with Prometheus and abandon absolute tyranny. So man too learns in the end the folly of misdoing, though it may take several generations of suffering to drive the lesson home. And the lesson which suffering teaches is not merely how to avoid suffering; it is how to do right, how to achieve justice. This is made clear in the third choral Ode in *Agamemnon*. Similarly in the second Ode the story of Paris, his proud wilfulness, his long defiance, and final overthrow, illustrates the slow but sure working of a moral universe, and prepares our minds for witnessing the same principle at work nearer home, in the family of Agamemnon. The sin of Atreus has to be expiated by his son; but the son too commits sin, by sacrificing his own daughter, and thus doubly justifies the fate

* See *Choephori*, p. 126, 'So to this day . . . our whole sex is cursed, by men disfranchised, scorned and portionless.'

which is prepared for him. Orestes is bound by immemorial tradition to exact vengeance for his murdered father; but his deed, even by the primitive standards of the old religion, is a still worse crime than that which he has avenged. In the end reconciliation is achieved. Just as Prometheus suffered for a thousand years, and then made terms with Zeus; so Orestes suffers torment at the hands of the Furies, and is at last granted release. Thus out of sin and struggle, revenge and atonement, there appears at last a new phase in man's quest for justice.

So the trilogy ends on a note of hopefulness and confidence; and in the final procession of *The Eumenides* Aeschylus, as it were, hands over to his fellow-citizens the issue of man's perpetual struggle with sin and vengeance, leaves with them the mystery of suffering and free-will. But the note of hopefulness is only the last note of a long and tragic tune, of which we learnt the refrain in *Agamemnon*: 'Cry Sorrow, sorrow – yet let good prevail!' The prayer answers the cry; but cry and prayer are both always present in the music of humanity. The prayer expresses a long hope for the future, inspired by contemplation of a long period of past suffering. Each man as philosopher or patriot may live by hope; but in his own flesh and spirit he knows neither past nor future, only the present:

> . . . But I must feel
> The parting of the flesh
> Before the whetted steel.

Though philosophy and patriotism end the drama in hope, human suffering and despair fill the more memorable scenes. The joy of the final Chorus does not refute the realism of Cassandra's parting words,

> And grief itself's hardly more pitiable than joy.

For it is only on rare occasions, such as the witnessing of transcendent drama in a unique religious setting, that men are raised by communion of emotion to regard life with the eyes of philosophers. Life itself is lived day by day, and suffering is not sublimated or dramatized but endured. The hopefulness of Aeschylus belongs partly to his own day, partly to those in every age who have the philosopher's vision;

but his despair, his knowledge of suffering and of courage – this is what makes his poetry as true for us as it was for his Athenians; for a large part of truth is necessarily tragic, and tragedy, the greatest of the literary arts, was the creation of Aeschylus.

## AGAMEMNON

The play opens with a brief scene in which a Watchman posted on the palace roof by Clytemnestra sees the beacon which announces the capture of Troy. There are two notes in his speech: hope, because Agamemnon may now be expected home; and foreboding, because of the unfaithfulness of the wife who awaits him. Then comes a long lyric passage in which the Chorus, Elders of Argos, express the same mixed feelings, with stronger emphasis on foreboding. It is not only Clytemnestra who arouses their fear – they trust Agamemnon to find a way to deal with her when he returns; but they know that the king himself is burdened with guilt. They recount in detail how Agamemnon, inheriting the family curse from Atreus, found himself faced with a fearful dilemma, and made the wrong choice – to sacrifice his daughter. They point out that Fate is not absolute: Fate confronts man with a choice, and if man chooses wrongly the sin is his.

> Then he put on
> The harness of Necessity.

Clytemnestra now comes to tell them that Troy is captured, and answers their incredulity with a description of the series of beacons she had posted to span a distance of some 400 miles. The Elders listen politely; and, carried away by her eloquence, seem to believe that her news is true. Then in a long choral Ode, they trace the hand of Zeus, which has revealed itself in so notable a punishment of sin – the sin of Paris in seducing Helen. From this sin has resulted, first, the utter destruction of the city and people of Troy; but the Chorus describe a secondary result, the sorrows they have known in Argos, the grief of the deserted king, Menelaus, and the resentment of the people of Greece at the slaughter of their men in a foreign war. Agamemnon will not come home to an easy situation. Success and glory are in themselves a danger. In the end, discouraged by this recurrence of foreboding, they reflect how improbable is Clytemnestra's story of the beacons, and decide to think no more of it.*

Here an interval takes place, representing the lapse of some days. The Chorus reassemble when Agamemnon's Herald arrives to announce his master's return. He describes the hardships of ten years, and the disastrous storms of the homeward voyage. The third choral Ode speaks of the beauty of Helen, and the terrible curse which followed her to Troy. But that curse expressed, not the gods' envy of mortal happiness, but their anger at mortal sin. Troy fell because, in the person of Paris, she sinned against the holy law which commands mutual trust and respect between host and guest. By refusing to give Helen back, Troy took this sin upon herself, and suffered for it. The Chorus are so deeply occupied with applying the law of retribution to Paris, that they forget the theme of the first Ode; its application to Agamemnon has faded from their minds, as the victorious king enters in his chariot, followed by a second chariot containing spoils of war, and Cassandra, the captive princess of Troy.

The Elders greet Agamemnon; and try, without being specific, to warn him that he may receive some welcomes less genuine than theirs. He replies in a tone of some self-satisfaction; and then Clytemnestra appears. Her speeches in this scene are packed with subtlety. Her welcome is fulsome in its protestation of love. Her reference to his ten years' absence, which should have sounded like a tender expression of sorrow, by a slight shift of emphasis becomes a bitter accusation of neglect. Every sentence is calculated to cause Agamemnon uneasiness, yet give him no shadow of excuse for expressing it. She harps on one theme – Agamemnon's death – the many deaths that rumour had given him in his absence. The eagerness with which she had awaited him is extravagantly drawn; and its effect is, as she intended, to awake distaste rather than suspicion. Then she calls upon her maids to spread a carpet of purple cloth from the chariot to the palace door, to receive the feet of the conqueror.

Agamemnon in reply snubs his wife resoundingly, and rebukes her for thus inviting the jealousy of the gods to fall on him. She accepts this without any hint of resentment, and rejoins with a flood of two-faced imagery which rouses in the audience an uneasiness to balance

* But see note on p. 185.

Agamemnon's. The sea, she says, is an inexhaustible source of purple dye; and Agamemnon can well afford to tread on expensive cloth. But the 'sea' she speaks of is the family feud, inexhaustible in hate; the 'purple dye' is blood shed for revenge; the 'one outpouring', the 'safe journey's end', are alike ambiguous. The 'unripe grape' is a word also used for a 'young virgin', and therefore means Iphigenia, from whose death springs the wrath of Zeus against her father; 'coolness' may be either a shelter from the heat, or the chill of death; and 'perfected' is the word used of an unblemished victim upon which all the rites preliminary to sacrifice have been performed. But Agamemnon, self-confident and contemptuous, listens without understanding. (See Appendix, page 195.)

Meanwhile Clytemnestra's maids have draped the floor and the steps with purple. Agamemnon refuses to set foot upon it. Clytemnestra cajoles, suggesting he is afraid. At last he graciously yields, has his boots removed by a slave, and treads on the purple cloth. Clytemnestra utters a shrill and terrifying cry of triumph, ostensibly to celebrate the king's victorious return, actually to mark the moment when she feels her own victory assured. Again she has caused uneasiness mounting to momentary terror for the Elders, until her apparent meaning convinces them; only Cassandra knows her real meaning. The king enters his palace. Clytemnestra remains behind for a brief prayer to Zeus, that he will bring her designs to fulfilment; then she too goes in.

This is a significant episode. By persuading Agamemnon against his better judgement to walk on purple to the altar where he himself is to be the 'perfected' victim, Clytemnestra achieves three things. First, she demonstrates her personal ascendancy over her husband; however he may disguise his weakness, he knows that he is in her hands. But his yielding is not only folly; it is sin. To a Greek the essence of piety was humility, the conscious acknowledgement that the gods are greater than man, and that man's greatness is held by their sufferance. Agamemnon in his first speech had arrogantly allowed Heaven a share in his glory as conqueror; to walk on purple would symbolize his appropriation of the whole glory of victory, and be a visible defiance of the gods. It is the kingly ambition of his nature which tempts him to make this visible claim before his wife and his subjects; it is his weakness that admits the momentary pretence, which he knows to be false, that such pride can escape divine anger. The second thing, then, that Clytemnestra achieves is the planting of conscious guilt in his heart. He is about to approach an altar to pray; and he will pray knowing that he addresses an offended deity. The third is the most important of all: this action demonstrates to Argos, and to the audience, that the man whose fall we are to witness is self-doomed; that he is by nature the kind of man who cannot survive in a world ruled by just and holy powers; that he is one whom the gods must inevitably destroy. This realization gives exact meaning to Clytemnestra's words,

Zeus, Zeus, Fulfiller! now fulfil these prayers of mine!

The Chorus, left alone, are now thoroughly aroused to the sense of impending catastrophe. Can evil not be averted? Yes – by one who is ready to pay due respect to the gods. But the king's lack of respect reminds them again that he is already in debt, for the blood of his own daughter. For the first time a suspicion of the truth touches them; but they dare not name so horrible a thing. At this point we are surprised by a reappearance of Clytemnestra, who comes to call on Cassandra to take her place with the rest of the household at the ritual cleansing that is about to be observed. Cassandra appears neither to see nor to hear her; and the queen retires, leaving the Elders to deal with her.

They already know her reputation as a prophetess. They now learn that this power was given her by Apollo himself, after she had promised to return his love. When she broke her promise, Apollo in anger doomed her to be always a true prophet and always disbelieved; but he still respected her virginity. At the fall of Troy Agamemnon asked for Cassandra as his share of the spoil; and what Apollo left untouched, Agamemnon violated.

Cassandra trembles, possessed by the prophet-god. She speaks of Thyestes' banquet, and sees the walls of the palace still dripping blood. She sees Agamemnon's death, and the sword in Clytemnestra's grasp, and describes her vision in lurid pictorial flashes which the Elders will not or dare not understand. She sees her own body lying dead beside the king's and weeps for her own pitiful fate; and still the Chorus are obtuse, though sympathetic. Then, abandoning lyrical ejaculation, she makes a supreme effort to control herself and speak clearly, in the ordinary blank verse of dialogue. She moves nearer to simple statement, and at last declares,

> I say Agamemnon shall lie dead before your eyes.

Immediately Apollo's curse operates: the Elders, who hitherto have inclined to belief, retreat in panic from plain truth. Cassandra turns from them to address Apollo, whom she accuses and defies as her destroyer, flinging off and trampling the sacred emblems with which he had invested her as his prophetess. She foretells the further progress of the curse, Orestes' vengeance upon Clytemnestra; and with a prayer for a quick death, and a short despairing elegy on all human happiness, goes into the palace.

Soon after, the death-shriek of the king is heard; the Elders debate rapidly what to do; and the palace doors open to reveal Clytemnestra standing over the bleeding corpses of Agamemnon and Cassandra.

The impact of Clytemnestra's exultant and defiant realism as she claims the carnage for her own handiwork cannot be paralleled for power by anything in ancient drama. A long altercation follows; as it proceeds, we begin at last to see behind the armour of ferocity something of the bitterness of suffering which has festered within her since Iphigenia was taken from her and killed; and something of the weariness which the strain of revenge has left behind. Clytemnestra may be a fiend, but she is also a woman. The Chorus are forced to admit that, though they must condemn her act, they cannot see where truth and justice lie; and at this point, to complicate still further the despairing search for justice, Aegisthus enters, and with his first words offers thanks to the just gods.

Aegisthus' character is described for us by the Elders as that of a coward who would not go with Agamemnon to the war, a lecher who seduced the king's wife, and again a coward who allowed a woman to wield the sword against his enemy. We must also look at the lines Aeschylus has given him to speak. His statements are free from boastfulness and from pretence, and his description of events is objective – as far as it goes; we notice, however, that when he speaks of the banishment of Thyestes by Atreus he omits to mention the reason –

that Thyestes had seduced Atreus' wife. For the rest, he makes no claim to be a hero; but as he tells – with a passionate precision which cannot fail to win some sympathy – the ghastly story of what Agamemnon's father did to his father Thyestes, we realize that the filial obligation which drove him to plot vengeance on the son of Atreus is exactly the same as that which now lies upon Orestes, which we shall see Orestes fulfil in the next play. There is then no point in branding Aegisthus coward because he did not go to fight in Agamemnon's war. The other two charges, of course, remain; but are they, taken together, a worse crime than matricide? or worse than the crime which Aegisthus had to avenge? The Chorus themselves admit that, unlike Clytemnestra, he refrains from insulting the dead king. His appeal is to justice, and his resolve is to rule. Aeschylus does not praise or excuse Aegisthus; but his insistence on presenting his case fairly ensures that the urgency of the central theme, What is justice? is still further heightened by the closing scene of the play. Challenged by the Elders, Aegisthus makes a show of force; Clytemnestra pleads for restraint; and the Elders withdraw, shouting threats and defiance.

## THE CHOEPHORI

### or THE LIBATION-BEARERS

Seven years have passed. Clytemnestra and Aegisthus have ruled Argos firmly, but have squandered the treasure that Agamemnon brought home from Troy. The people are cowed and resentful. Clytemnestra's daughter, Electra, who some time before Agamemnon's return conveyed Orestes safely out of Argos and sent him to relatives in Phocis, has continued her defiance of her mother, and is now reduced to a condition of life hardly different from that of a slave, unmarried, hoping only for Orestes' return. Agamemnon's body, refused funeral honours, lies under a plain mound of earth outside the city walls.

The text of the opening speech is defective; but the drift is clear. Orestes, now a man, is standing, in the dusk before dawn, at his father's tomb, to seek his aid and blessing in the duty of revenge which he has returned to undertake. He soon sees Electra coming with some female slaves from the palace, bringing libations of wine to offer at the tomb to the spirits of the dead. He conceals himself, learns by listening why the 'Libation-Bearers' have come; then appears, makes himself known to his sister, and with her plots the murder of Clytemnestra and Aegisthus.

Orestes and Electra are not characters in the same full sense as Clytemnestra and Agamemnon in the first play. The one fact known about Orestes, that he was commanded by a god to kill his mother, is so absorbing in its terror that it leaves no room in the portrait of him for incidental features. He is an instrument in Apollo's ruthless hand, a stage in man's moral pilgrimage, a battle-ground where justice joins issue with pity and humanity. The consciousness of his mission has filled his mind for a long time. He has brooded on his father's death, his own deprivation and exile, his mother's wickedness, and the penalties that will afflict him if he neglects a son's duty. He suffers the more because he is not hardened, but feels to the full the claim of a mother upon her son. He courageously accepts what Fate has laid upon him; and in the final play we feel that it is his heroic suffering that completes the expiation of the curse, and vindicates the justice of the ultimate settlement.

In the same way Electra's personal situation is simple and complete, a depth of misery and humiliation lit by a single hope, her brother's return and vengeance. It is this situation which governs every word and act; all that is required in the way of character is an unswerving resolution, and this Electra has. After the long first scene she does not appear again, nor indeed is she mentioned*. There is no word in Aeschylus of the romantic tradition that she married her cousin Pylades, who appears here as Orestes' companion and friend.

The Chorus, who are slaves of the palace and intimate with Electra, play a remarkable part in the planning and accomplishment of the revenge. It is they who encourage Electra at first to pray for the violent deaths of Aegisthus and Clytemnestra. As soon as they recognize Orestes they encourage him to action, and place themselves under his orders. They persuade the Nurse to tell Aegisthus to come without his armed escort. The doubt and abhorrence which torture Orestes do not exist for them, either before or after the deed is done.

* But see note on p. 191.

Their outlook is that of the chthonian religion, modified by reliance on Apollo for his promised purification.

To return to the action of the play. At this point begins a very long lyric section in which Orestes, Electra, and the Chorus alternate in a series of stanzas, partly invocatory, partly reminiscent, whose purpose is to awake the anger of Agamemnon's spirit, and of the powers of the lower world, until they rise to help Orestes in his undertaking. There is a general crescendo of excitement extending over twenty-two stanzas, followed by shorter antiphonal sentences which seem to goad Agamemnon to revenge by recital of his humiliation. The great length of this passage provokes fascinating speculation on the original method of production, and on the use then made of music and choreography; a modern producer will almost certainly play safe, and cut it considerably. When it is concluded the action again gathers pace. The narrative of Clytemnestra's dream completes the hints given in the opening Ode; and the plot is laid: Orestes and Pylades will come disguised as foreign traders, and gain admittance to the palace by bringing news of Orestes – that he is dead.

The stage proper is now left empty; and the Chorus reflect, with some narrative, on the fearful crimes of which women are capable when roused by reckless passion. Then a new scene is revealed, and Orestes at the palace door is confronted by his mother. He tells his tale; is hospitably welcomed – 'As our guest, call this your home'; and with Pylades enters the palace.

Clytemnestra's part in this play is too short to allow of any real development beyond the fully conceived character already presented in *Agamemnon*. Naturally the Nurse, who is at one with the Chorus in hating Clytemnestra, assumes that she rejoices at heart to hear of Orestes' death; but the Nurse may well be as much mistaken in this as in her second assumption, that Clytemnestra has arranged to have her son murdered. On receiving the news from the supposed 'commercial traveller', the queen makes a show of grief whose wordy metaphors are as unconvincing as Macbeth's on the discovery of the dead Duncan; but even if her grief were real its expression in the circumstances could hardly sound anything but forced. The truth is that the process of helpless corruption, which the Argive Elders traced in the story of Paris, has worked itself out in Clytemnestra.

Seven years of usurpation, suspicion, and guilt have enfolded the once heroic outline in a cloud of obscurity; freedom has vanished in fear, and character in automatic reaction. One nobleness is allowed her at the end, which was given also to Cassandra: the woman, unlike the man, receives her death in silence.

The final scene is remarkable chiefly for the dramatic use which Aeschylus makes of the robe in which Clytemnestra had snared Agamemnon. This robe is mentioned in many allusions to the story, but only here explained. It seems to have been a voluminous bath-gown with cords threaded through loops so that they could be jerked tight in a moment; and this 'strait-jacket' Clytemnestra had designed and made herself, and kept in readiness for the day. A returning warrior must cleanse himself from the blood of those he had killed in war. For this ritual he would stand naked; his wife would attend, and throw a gown over him as he stepped from the bath to the altar, where an animal would wait ready for sacrifice, and near it the sacrificial sword. Agamemnon, his arms and legs pinioned by this 'neat device', had had no chance either to resist or to escape when Clytemnestra lifted the sword. The robe, pierced and blood-stained, had been kept – possibly by loyal slaves to whom Clytemnestra had entrusted the perfunctory burial. Orestes now makes his attendants hold it up, and turn it round; and by thus displaying its fiendish ingenuity he brings the murderous act vividly before his witnesses. Then side by side with the bodies of Agamemnon's murderers he lays the last robe which Agamemnon wore in life, and over it pronounces a son's farewell.

The end of the scene foreshadows the third play and the expiation of the curse. 'The third, completing draught' of blood has now been shed. Here an analogy is implied to the 'three libations' (the first to the Olympian gods, the second to the ancient heroes, the third to Zeus the Saviour) which by convivial tradition concluded the eating of a banquet and began the drinking. Now blood has been shed in three generations: by Atreus, by Agamemnon and Clytemnestra, and lastly by Orestes. The third libation is to the Saviour. The play ends with the question, Will Zeus now save this tormented house, and bring the curse to an end?

## THE EUMENIDES

Hitherto the whole story has been intensely concerned with human actions, with human fate and human feelings. At the same time the pattern of events has been shown as the reflection of a pattern of divine will, as the working-out of divinely ordained moral principles. Zeus is in heaven, judging sin and forgetting nothing; Apollo is in his temple, where his unearthly voice commanded Orestes to act as the instrument of retribution. Man is now at the limit of despair and suffering; it is time for gods to appear and speak.

The scene shows the front of Apollo's temple at Delphi. It is early morning, and the Priestess is about to enter. She invokes all the gods, old and new, who have held this shrine from the earliest ages; then passes through the doorway. A moment later the solemn silence is broken by her terrified cries, and she staggers out, hardly able to tell what she has seen. Inside the temple a blood-stained murderer crouches by the altar; and round him, all asleep with weariness, lie the Furies, not now invisible, but a sight to horrify piety and melt courage. Aghast at this pollution of Apollo's shrine, the Priestess withdraws. The temple-façade is rolled aside, and we see what we have heard described; but there are also two figures whom the Priestess did not see. Apollo himself stands by Orestes, and near him is his brother Hermes, the god of journeys. Apollo speaks; comforts and encourages Orestes; and sends him, with Hermes as escort, to seek final deliverance in Athens.

The Furies are left alone, still sleeping; and in their midst appears suddenly another figure, not recognized at first; until she lifts the pale and haggard face of Clytemnestra. Her voice is the piteous whisper of a ghost, and she tries to wake the Furies with passionate reproaches. As they stir, she vanishes; and soon the whole pack of loathsome monsters springs into life, enraged at the escape of their prey. Now Apollo appears again, to drive them from his sacred floor. His eloquent indignation forgets – nor do the Furies remind him – that they are the same fiends with whose torments Apollo had threatened Orestes, if he failed to avenge his father. Apollo now tells them that Orestes is to be tried by Athene in Athens; and bids them go too, and state their case before her.

The scene changes again, to show Orestes clinging for sanctuary to an altar in Athene's temple in Athens. The Furies arrive and find him; and they recite an impressive Ode which is partly a statement of their eternal function of punishment, and partly a spell-binding song to secure their victim. Athene herself now enters; hears briefly the pleas of accusers and accused; and goes to summon the wisest of her citizens to sit as a judicial court. The Furies, sure of their right, agree to a trial. While the court is being summoned, in a further Ode they pronounce an urgent warning against the dangers of leniency towards crime, and forecast the rise of a 'new wickedness', unknown in former ages when wholesome fear guided men's ways and enforced good behaviour. Moreover, they insist that good behaviour in itself is not enough; it must spring from goodness of heart. They end with a picture of the shipwreck suffered by the man who stubbornly resists the authority of justice. Then twelve Athenian Elders arrive, the court of Areopagus is solemnly constituted, and the pleading begins.

The leader of the Chorus questions Orestes to establish the fact that he killed his mother at Apollo's command. Orestes is soon at a loss, and calls on Apollo to conduct the case for him. In order that this scene may have its full dramatic effect, it must become evident that the problem is too hard for human solution. The hideousness of the Furies, their blind unreason and ferocity, dispose the audience against them; and Orestes' case at first sight seems strong. But Apollo now makes four speeches, in each of which, impressive though they may sound at first, he betrays the inadequacy of his position.*

First, he says that his oracles are not his, but all delivered at the express command of Zeus. To begin with, this implies an appeal to authority rather than to reason, an approach which may well be unpleasing to the Athenian audience. Further, Apollo invites the judges to regard the will of Zeus as weightier than the oath they have

---

* It should be noted also that Apollo's record in the first two plays makes him a suspect witness. He is reproached by the Herald (p. 61) for enmity to the Greek army at Troy; he is denounced by Cassandra (p. 86) for heartless cruelty; and he is the instigator of matricide, which no insistence on justice can make tolerable.

taken to judge according to their understanding; a suggestion certain to arouse mistrust. Lastly, Apollo claims the authority of Zeus for all his oracles, both personal *and political*. Now, Delphi was notoriously pro-Persian at the time of the Persian invasion; and if Apollo can mistake in politics, why not in morals?

Apollo's second speech asserts that Agamemnon's death was not to be compared with Clytemnestra's, because Agamemnon was a man and a king, and his wife killed by treachery. But Apollo had commanded Orestes (see *Choephori*, p. 139) to kill Clytemnestra by treachery; and his valuation of the two deaths completely ignores the added horror attaching to matricide. Further, the phrase 'for the most part successful' hints strongly at the part which was disastrous, the sacrifice of Iphigenia, and thus reminds the audience of Agamemnon's guilt and Clytemnestra's excuse.

His third speech, begun with violent invective, is a still weaker argument, and by emphasizing the finality of murder plays into the Furies' hands; for the murder of a woman is as final as that of a man.

Lastly, Apollo puts forward a far-fetched theory of parenthood: 'the mother is not the true parent of the child; she is a nurse who tends the growth of young seed', and so on. This again cannot possibly make a clear appeal to any audience, for it denies outright the intimate bond between mother and child. Apollo's plea ends with the promise of many gifts to make Athens great; and this, the open offering of a bribe to an Athenian court, should finally dispose of any doubt that Aeschylus has intended to present Apollo's case as, at the best, unsatisfactory. The Chorus-leader answers with a single sentence bidding the judges reverence their oath, i.e., judge according to their conscience rather than in fear of the will of Zeus as interpreted by Apollo.

Athene then announces the perpetual constitution of the court of Areopagus, and bids the citizens (as the Chorus have already bidden them) enthrone fear as the great safeguard of law. Should the votes be equal, she says, her casting vote will be given for Orestes. This is what happens. The case is too hard for human decision; matricide is a fearful crime, against which must be set both the divine command and the long period of suffering and ritual cleansing that Orestes has undergone. Athene's vote comes into effect; and Orestes, with a solemn pledge of eternal friendship between Argos and Athens, leaves the court a free man.

It remains for Athene to calm the resentment and avert the threats of the Furies. She insists that the trial has been fair; that the even voting means that the Furies are neither defeated nor disgraced; that the position offered to them in Athens assures them perpetual honour and usefulness. Finally they relent, and pronounce blessings instead of curses. Thus violence retires, and 'holy Persuasion', the civilizing instrument of the new age, wins the day. The great Panathenaic procession gathers on the stage, and with the Chorus passes out through the orchestra.

## THE TEXT

For *Agamemnon* I have used the edition of Professor A. Y. Campbell, whose work on the very corrupt text of the greatest of all Greek plays seems to me an achievement for which only the future can render suitable thanks. I have also been able, through his help, to take advantage of many notes that he has published in various periodicals since his edition appeared in 1936; so that this is a translation of a text which will not in fact exist complete in print until the appearance of the next revised edition of Professor Campbell's work.

For *The Choephori* I have used the edition of Professor T. G. Tucker, and for *The Eumenides* the 'Oxford Text' edited by A. Sidgwick, with some reference in difficult passages to Professor G. Thomson's *Oresteia*.

## THE TRANSLATION

This is not a very literal translation. Several extremely good and fairly literal translations are available, from which the reader who knows some Greek may guess at the phrase used in the original, and the reader who knows none may gather a vague but perhaps impressive glimpse of a vanished language. I have tried rather to concentrate on fullness of meaning, interpretation, and suitability for performance; not attempting to represent either the peculiarities of Greek poetic diction or the highly individual style of Aeschylus, but hoping for a direct, unconditional impact. Neither have I attempted to reproduce any Greek rhythms or metrical patterns. Most of these belong essentially to an inflexional language, and change their character when adapted to English. Instead I have used the disciplines native to our tongue: simple, strongly marked metres, and rhyme. And in the lyric portions, where the writing is pictorial, compressed, and full of double meaning, I have sometimes expanded for the sake of clarity; occasionally, where an explanatory phrase or line has been added, this is mentioned in the notes. Such expansion, however, is mainly confined to *Agamemnon*, where many obscurities are made still more obscure by textual corruption.

The highest ideal of a translation from Greek is achieved when the reader flings it impatiently into the fire, and begins patiently to learn the language for himself.

P.H.V.

NOTE

The line numbers in this edition refer to the lines of the original Greek text.

# AGAMEMNON

# AGAMEMNON

\*

## CHARACTERS:

A WATCHMAN
CHORUS *of twelve Elders of Argos*
CLYTEMNESTRA, *wife of Agamemnon*
A HERALD
AGAMEMNON, *king of Argos*
CASSANDRA, *a princess of Troy*
AEGISTHUS, *Clytemnestra's paramour, cousin to Agamemnon*
*Soldiers attending Agamemnon; guards attending Aegisthus*

\*

*It is night, a little before sunrise. On the roof of Atreus' palace a*
WATCHMAN *stands, or rises from a small mattress placed on the*
*hewn stone. In front of the palace are statues of Zeus, Apollo, and*
*Hermes; each with an altar before it.*

WATCHMAN: O gods! grant me release from this long weary
    watch.
Release, O gods! Twelve full months now, night after night
Dog-like I lie here, keeping guard from this high roof
On Atreus' palace. The nightly conference of stars,
Resplendent rulers, bringing heat and cold in turn,
Studding the sky with beauty – I know them all, and watch
    them
Setting and rising; but the one light I long to see
Is a new star, the promised sign, the beacon-flare
To speak from Troy and utter one word, 'Victory!' –
Great news for Clytemnestra, in whose woman's heart
A man's will nurses hope.

Now once more, drenched with dew,
I walk about; lie down, but no dreams visit me.
Sleep's enemy, fear, stands guard beside me, to forbid
My eyes one instant's closing. If I sing some tune –
Since music's the one cure prescribed for heartsickness –
Why, then I weep, to think how changed this house is now
From splendour of old days, ruled by its rightful lord.
So may the gods be kind and grant release from trouble,
And send the fire to cheer this dark night with good news.

*The beacon shines out.*

O welcome beacon, kindling night to glorious day,
Welcome! You'll set them dancing in every street in Argos
When they hear your message. Ho there! Hullo! Call
    Clytemnestra!
The Queen must rise at once like Dawn from her bed, and
    welcome
The fire with pious words and a shout of victory,
For the town of Ilion's ours – that beacon's clear enough!
I'll be the first myself to start the triumphal dance.
Now I can say the gods have blessed my master's hand;
And for me too that beacon-light's a lucky throw.
Now Heaven bring Agamemnon safe to his home! May I
Hold his dear hand in mine! For the rest, I say no more;
My tongue's nailed down. This house itself, if walls had
    words,
Would tell its story plainly. Well, I speak to those
Who understand me; to the rest – my door is shut.

*He descends. Lights begin to appear in the palace. A cry of triumph
is heard from* CLYTEMNESTRA *within, and is echoed by other
women. Then from the palace a messenger hurries out towards the
city; attendants follow, going in various directions, and carrying
jars and bowls with oil and incense for sacrifice. Then*
CLYTEMNESTRA *enters from the palace, with two attendants;*

42

*she casts incense on the altars, and prays before the statue of Zeus.*
    *Day begins to break. From the city enter the* ELDERS OF
ARGOS. *They do not yet see* CLYTEMNESTRA.

CHORUS: Ten years have passed since the strong sons of
    Atreus,
  Menelaus and Agamemnon, both alike
  Honoured by Zeus with throned and sceptred power,
  Gathered and manned a thousand Argive ships,
  And with the youth of Hellas under arms
  Sailed from these ports to settle scores with Priam.

  Then loud their warlike anger cried,
  As eagles cry, that wild with grief,
  On some steep, lonely mountain-side
  Above their robbed nest wheel and sail,
  Oaring the airy waves, and wail
  Their wasted toil, their watchful pride;
  Till some celestial deity,
  Zeus, Pan, Apollo, hears on high
  Their scream of wordless misery;
  And pitying their forlorn estate
  (Since air is Heaven's protectorate)
  Sends a swift Fury to pursue
  Marauding guilt with vengeance due.

  So against Paris's guilty boast
  Zeus, witness between guest and host,
  Sends Atreus' sons for stern redress
  Of his and Helen's wantonness.
  Now Greece and Troy both pay their equal debt
  Of aching limbs and wounds and sweat,
  While knees sink low in gory dust,
  And spears are shivered at first thrust.

Things are – as they are now; their end
Shall follow Fate's decree, which none can bend.
In vain shall Priam's altars burn,
His rich libations vainly flow
To gods above and powers below:
No gift, no sacrificial flame
Can soothe or turn
The wrath of Heaven from its relentless aim.

We were too old to take our share
With those who joined the army then.
We lean on sticks – in strength not men
But children; so they left us here.
In weakness youth and age are one:
The sap sleeps in the unripe bone
As in the withered. The green stalk
Grows without thorns: so, in the grey
And brittle years, old men must walk
Three-footed, weak as babes, and stray
Like dreams lost in the light of day.

*Here the* CHORUS-LEADER *sees* CLYTEMNESTRA.

Daughter of Tyndareos, Queen Clytemnestra,
What have you heard? What has happened? Why have you
    ordered
Sacrifice through the city? Is there news?
Altars of all the gods who guard our State,
Gods of the sky, powers of the lower earth,
Altars of town and country, blaze with offerings;
On every hand heaven-leaping flames implore
Anger to melt in gentleness – a glare
Enriched with holy ointment, balm so rare
As issues only from a royal store!

44

Why are these things? Be gracious, Queen:
Tell what you can, or what you may;
Be healer of this haunting fear
Which now like an enemy creeps near,
And now again, when hope has seen
These altars bright with promise, slinks away —
Tell us, that hope may lift the load
Which galls our souls by night and day,
Sick with the evil which has been,
The evil which our hearts forebode.

CLYTEMNESTRA *remains silent, her back turned to the* CHORUS.

*They continue, addressing the audience.*

I am the man to speak, if you would hear
The whole tale from its hopeful starting-place —
That portent, which amazed our marching youth.
It was ten years ago — but I was there.
The poet's grace, the singer's fire,
Grow with his years; and I can still speak truth
With the clear ring the gods inspire; —
How those twin monarchs of our warlike race,
Two leaders one in purpose, were sped forth —
Their vengeful spears in thousands pointing North
To Troy — by four wings' furious beat:
Two kings of birds, that seemed to bode
Great fortune to the kings of that great fleet.
Close to the palace, on spear-side of the road,
One tawny-feathered, one white in the tail,
Perched in full view, they ravenously tear
The body of a pregnant hare
Big with her burden, now a living prey
In the last darkness of their unborn day.
*Cry Sorrow, sorrow — yet let good prevail!*

45

The army's learned Seer saw this, and knew
The devourers of the hare
For that relentless pair –
Different in nature, as the birds in hue –
The sons of Atreus; and in council of war
Thus prophesied: 'Your army, it is true,
In time shall make King Priam's town their prey;
Those flocks and herds Troy's priests shall slay
With prayers for safety of her wall
Perish in vain – Troy's violent doom shall swallow all.
Only, see to it, you who go
To bridle Trojan pride, that no
Anger of gods benight your day
And strike before your hulls are under way.
For virgin Artemis, whom all revere,
Hates with a deadly hate
The swift-winged hounds of Zeus who swooped to assail
Their helpless victim wild with fear
Before her ripe hour came;
Who dared to violate
(So warning spoke the priest)
The awe that parenthood must claim,
As for some rite performed in Heaven's name;
Yes, Artemis abominates the eagles' feast!'
*Cry Sorrow, sorrow – yet let good prevail!*

Still spoke on the prophet's tongue:
'Lovely child of Zeus, I pray,
You who love the tender whelp
Of the ravening lion, and care
For the fresh-wild sucking young
Of fox and rat and hind and hare;
If ever by your heavenly help
Hope of good was brought to flower,

46

Bless the sign we saw today!
Cancel all its presaged ill,
All its promised good fulfil!
Next my anxious prayers entreat
Lord Apollo's healing power,
That his Sister may not plan
Winds to chain the Hellene fleet;
That her grievance may not crave
Blood to drench another grave
From a different sacrifice
Hallowed by no festal joy –
Blood that builds a tower of hate,
Mad blood raging to destroy
Its self-source, a ruthless Fate
Warring with the flesh of man;
Bloodshed bringing in its train
Kindred blood that flows again,
Anger still unreconciled
Poisoning a house's life
With darkness, treachery and strife,
Wreaking vengeance for a murdered child.'

So Calchas, from that parting prodigy
Auguring the royal house's destiny,
Pronounced his warning of a fatal curse,
With hope of better mingling fear of worse.
Let us too, echoing his uncertain tale,
Cry *Sorrow, sorrow – yet let good prevail!*

Let good prevail!
So be it! Yet, what is good? And who
Is God? How name him, and speak true?
If he accept the name that men
Give him, Zeus I name him then.

47

I, still perplexed in mind,
For long have searched and weighed
Every hope of comfort or of aid:
Still I can find
No creed to lift this heaviness,
This fear that haunts without excuse –
No name inviting faith, no wistful guess,
Save only – Zeus.

The first of gods is gone,
Old Ouranos, once blown
With violence and pride;
His name shall not be known,
Nor that his dynasty once lived, and died.
His strong successor, Cronos, had his hour,
Then went his way, thrice thrown
By a yet stronger power.
Now Zeus is lord; and he
Who loyally acclaims his victory
Shall by heart's instinct find the universal key:

Zeus, whose will has marked for man
The sole way where wisdom lies;
Ordered one eternal plan:
*Man must suffer to be wise.*
Head-winds heavy with past ill
Stray his course and cloud his heart:
Sorrow takes the blind soul's part –
Man grows wise against his will.
For powers who rule from thrones above
By ruthlessness commend their love.

So was it then. Agamemnon, mortified,
Dared not, would not, admit to error; thought

Of his great Hellene fleet, and in his pride
Spread sail to the ill wind he should have fought.
Meanwhile his armed men moped along the shores,
And cursed the wind, and ate his dwindling stores;
Stared at white Chalkis' roofs day after day
Across the swell that churned in Aulis Bay.
And still from Strymon came that Northern blast,
While hulks and ropes grew rotten, moorings parted,
Deserters slunk away,
All ground their teeth, bored, helpless, hungry, thwarted.
The days of waiting doubled. More days passed.
The flower of warlike Hellas withered fast.

Then Calchas spoke again. The wind, he said,
Was sent by Artemis; and he revealed
Her remedy – a thought to crush like lead
The hearts of Atreus' sons, who wept, as weep they must,
And speechless ground their sceptres in the dust.

The elder king then spoke: 'What can I say?
Disaster follows if I disobey;
Surely yet worse disaster if I yield
And slaughter my own child, my home's delight,
In her young innocence, and stain my hand
With blasphemous unnatural cruelty,
Bathed in the blood I fathered! Either way,
Ruin! Disband the fleet, sail home, and earn
The deserter's badge – abandon my command,
Betray the alliance – now? The wind must turn,
There must be sacrifice, a maid must bleed –
Their chafing rage demands it – they are right!
May good prevail, and justify my deed!'

Then he put on
The harness of Necessity.

The doubtful tempest of his soul
Veered, and his prayer was turned to blasphemy,
His offering to impiety.
Hence that repentance late and long
Which, since his madness passed, pays toll
For that one reckless wrong.
Shameless self-willed infatuation
Emboldens men to dare damnation,
And starts the wheels of doom which roll
Relentless to their piteous goal.

So Agamemnon, rather than retreat,
Endured to offer up his daughter's life
To help a war fought for a faithless wife
And pay the ransom for a storm-bound fleet.

Heedless of her tears,
Her cries of 'Father!' and her maiden years,
Her judges valued more
Their glory and their war.
A prayer was said. Her father gave the word.
Limp in her flowing dress
The priest's attendants held her high
Above the altar, as men hold a kid.
Her father spoke again, to bid
One bring a gag, and press
Her sweet mouth tightly with a cord,
Lest Atreus' house be cursed by some ill-omened cry.

Rough hands tear at her girdle, cast
Her saffron silks to earth. Her eyes
Search for her slaughterers; and each,
Seeing her beauty, that surpassed
A painter's vision, yet denies

The pity her dumb looks beseech,
Struggling for voice; for often in old days,
When brave men feasted in her father's hall,
With simple skill and pious praise
Linked to the flute's pure tone
Her virgin voice would melt the hearts of all,
Honouring the third libation near her father's throne.

The rest I did not see,
Nor do I speak of it . . .
           But this I know:
What Calchas prophesies will be fulfilled.
The scale of Justice falls in equity:
The killer will be killed.

But now, farewell foreboding! Time may show,
But cannot alter, what shall be.
What help, then, to bewail
Troubles before they fall?
Events will take their way
Even as the prophet's words foreshadowed all.
For what is next at hand,
Let good prevail!
That is the prayer we pray —
We, who alone now stand
In Agamemnon's place, to guard this Argive land.

*The day has broken.* THE QUEEN *now turns and stands*
*facing the* ELDERS.

CHORUS: We come obedient to your bidding, Clytemnestra.
   Our king and leader absent, and his throne unfilled,
   Our duty pays his due observance to his wife.
   Have you received some message? Do these sacrifices
   Rise for good news, give thanks for long hope re-assured?
   I ask in love; and will as loyally receive
   Answer or silence.

CLYTEMNESTRA: Good news, if the proverb's true,
   Should break with sunrise from the kindly womb of night.
   But here's a richer joy than you dared ever hope:
   Our Argive men have captured Priam's town.

CHORUS:                                              Have *what*?
   I heard it wrong – I can't believe it!

CLYTEMNESTRA:                          Troy is ours!
   Is that clear speaking?

CHORUS:                    Happiness fills my eyes with tears.

CLYTEMNESTRA: They show your loyalty.

CHORUS:                          Have you some sure proof of this?

CLYTEMNESTRA: I have indeed; unless a god has played me
   false.

CHORUS: A god! Was it some dream you had, persuaded
   you?

CLYTEMNESTRA: Dream! Am I one to air drowsy imaginings?

CHORUS: Surely you feed yourself on unconfirmed report?

CLYTEMNESTRA: You choose to criticize me as an ignorant
   girl!

CHORUS: Well, then, when was Troy captured?

CLYTEMNESTRA:                              In this very night
   That brought to birth this glorious sun.

CHORUS:                              What messenger
   Could fly so fast from Troy to here?

CLYTEMNESTRA:                      The god of fire!
   Ida first launched his blazing beam; thence to this palace
   Beacon lit beacon in relays of flame. From Ida

52

To Hermes' crag on Lemnos; from that island, third
To receive the towering torch was Athos, rock of Zeus;
There, as the blaze leapt the dark leagues, the watch in
   welcome
Leapt too, and a twin tower of brightness speared the
   sky,
Pointing athwart the former course; and in a stride
Crossing the Aegean, like the whip-lash of lightning, flew
The resinous dazzle, molten-gold, till the fish danced,
As at sunrise, enraptured with the beacon's glow,
Which woke reflected sunrise on Makistos' heights.
The watchman there, proof against sleep, surprise or sloth,
Rose faithful to the message; and his faggots' flame
Swept the wide distance to Euripus' channel, where
Its burning word was blazoned to the Messapian guards.
They blazed in turn, kindling their pile of withered heath,
And passed the signal on. The strong beam, still undimmed,
Crossed at one bound Asopus' plain, and like the moon
In brilliance, lighted on Cithaeron's crags, and woke
Another watch, to speed the flying token on.
On still the hot gleam hurtled, past Gorgopis' lake;
Made Aegiplanctus, stirred those watching mountaineers
Not to stint boughs and brushwood; generously they fed
Their beacon, and up burst a monstrous beard of fire,
Leapt the proud headland fronting the Saronic Gulf,
To lofty Arachnaeus, neighbour to our streets;
Thence on this Atreid palace the triumphant fire
Flashed, lineal descendant of the flame of Ida.

Such, Elders, was the ritual race my torchbearers,
Each at his faithful post succeeding each, fulfilled;
And first and last to run share equal victory.
Such, Elders, is my proof and token offered you,
A message sent to me from Troy by Agamemnon.

CHORUS: Madam, we will in due course offer thanks to
    Heaven;
  But now we want to savour wonder to the full,
  And hear you speak at length: tell us your news again!
CLYTEMNESTRA: Today the Greeks hold Troy! Her walls
    echo with cries
  That will not blend. Pour oil and vinegar in one vessel,
  You'll see them part and swirl, and never mix: so, there,
  I think, down narrow streets a discord grates the ear –
  Screams of the captured, shouts of those who've captured
    them,
  The unhappy and the happy. Women of Troy prostrate
  Over dead husbands, brothers; aged grandfathers
  Mourning dead sons and grandsons, and remembering
  Their very cries are slaves' cries now. . . . And then the
    victors:
  After a night of fighting, roaming, plundering,
  Hungry to breakfast, while their hosts lie quiet in dust;
  No rules to keep, no order of place; each with the luck
  That fell to him, quartered in captured homes of Troy,
  Tonight, at last, rolled in dry blankets, safe from frost –
  No going on guard–blissfully they'll sleep from dusk to dawn.

  If in that captured town they are reverencing the gods
  Whose home it was, and not profaning holy places,
  The victors will avoid being vanquished in their turn.
  Only, let no lust of unlawful plunder tempt
  Our soldiers' hearts with wealth, to their own harm – there
    still
  Remains the journey home: God grant we see them safe!
  If the fleet sails free from the taint of sin, the gods
  May grant them safely to retrace their outward course –
  Those whom no wakeful anger of the forgotten dead
  Waits to surprise with vengeance. . . .

# THE EUMENIDES

These are a woman's words.
May good prevail beyond dispute, in sight of all!
My life holds many blessings; I would enjoy them now.

CHORUS: Madam, your words are like a man's, both wise and
     kind.
Now we have heard trustworthy proof from your own lips,
We will prepare ourselves again to praise the gods,
Whose gracious acts call for our most devout response.

CLYTEMNESTRA *goes into the palace.*

CHORUS: Zeus, supreme of heavenly powers!
     Friendly night, whose fateful hours
     Built for Argos' warlike name
     Bright imperishable fame!
     Night in which a net was laid
     Fast about the Trojan towers
     Such that none of mortal flesh,
     Great or little, could evade
     Grim annihilation's deadly mesh!
     This is the hand of Zeus! Zeus we revere,
     Whose lasting law both host and guest must fear;
     Who long since against Paris bent
     His bow with careful aim, and sent
     His vengeance flying not too near
     Nor past the stars, but timed to pay
     The debt of Justice on the appointed day.

     'The hand of Zeus has cast
     The proud from their high place!'
     This we may say, and trace
     That hand from first to last.
     As Zeus foreknowing willed,
     So was their end fulfilled.

     One said, 'The gods disdain
     To mark man's wanton way

55

Who tramples in the dust
Beauty of holy things.'
Impious! The truth shows plain:
Pride now has paid its debt, and they
Who laughed at Right and put their boastful trust
In arms and swollen wealth of kings,
Have gone their destined way.
A middle course is best,
Not poor nor proud; but this,
By no clear rule defined,
Eludes the unstable, undiscerning mind,
Whose aim will surely miss.
Thenceforth there is no way to turn aside;
When man has once transgressed,
And in his wealth and pride
Spurned the high shrine of Justice, nevermore
May his sin hope to hide
In that safe dimness he enjoyed before.

Retreat cut off, the fiend Temptation
Forces him onward, the unseen
Effectual agent of Damnation;
When his fair freshness once has been
Blotched and defiled with grime, and he,
Like worthless bronze, which testing blows
Have blackened, lies despoiled, and shows
His baseness plain for all to see,
Then every cure renews despair;
A boy chasing a bird on wing,
He on his race and soil must bring
A deeper doom than flesh can bear;
The gods are deaf to every prayer;
If pity lights a human eye,
Pity by Justice' law must share
The sinner's guilt, and with the sinner die.

So, doomed, deluded, Paris came
To sit at his host's table, and seduce
Helen his wife, and shame
The house of Atreus and the law of Zeus.

Bequeathing us in Argos
Muster of shields and spears,
The din of forge and dockyard,
Lightly she crossed the threshold
And left her palace, fearless
Of what should wake her fears;
And took to Troy as dowry
Destruction, blood, and tears.
Here, in her home deserted,
The voice of guard and groom
With love and grief lamented:
'O house! O king! O pity!
O pillow softly printed
Where her loved head had rested!'
There lies her husband fasting,
Dumb in his stricken room.
His thought across sea reaches
With longings, not reproaches;
A ghost will rule the palace,
A home become a tomb!
Her statue's sweet perfection
Torments his desolation;
Still his eyes' hunger searches –
That living grace is hardened
And lost that beauty's bloom.

Visions of her beset him
With false and fleeting pleasure
When dreams and dark are deep.

He sees her, runs to hold her;
And, through his fingers slipping,
Lightly departs his treasure,
The dream he cannot keep,
Wafted on wings that follow
The shadowy paths of sleep.

Such are the searching sorrows
This royal palace knows,
While through the streets of Argos
Grief yet more grievous grows,
With all our manhood gathered
So far from earth of Hellas;
As in each home unfathered,
Each widowed bed, the whetted
Sword of despair assails
Hearts where all hope has withered
And angry hate prevails.
They sent forth men to battle,
But no such men return;
And home, to claim their welcome,
Come ashes in an urn.

For War's a banker, flesh his gold.
There by the furnace of Troy's field,
Where thrust meets thrust, he sits to hold
His scale, and watch the spear-point sway;
And back to waiting homes he sends
Slag from the ore, a little dust
To drain hot tears from hearts of friends;
Good measure, safely stored and sealed
In a convenient jar – the just
Price for the man they sent away.
They praise him through their tears, and say,

'He was a soldier!' or, 'He died
Nobly, with death on every side!'
And fierce resentment mutters low,
'Yes – for another's wife!' And so
From grief springs gall, which fear must hide –
Let kings and their revenges go!
But under Ilion's wall the dead,
Heirs of her earth, lie chambered deep;
While she, whose living blood they shed,
Covers her conquerors in sleep.

A nation's voice, enforced with anger,
Strikes deadly as a public curse.
I wait for word of hidden danger,
And fear lest bad give place to worse.
God marks that man with watchful eyes
Who counts his killed by companies;
And when his luck, his proud success,
Forgets the law of righteousness,
Then the dark Furies launch at length
A counter-blow to crush his strength
And cloud his brightness, till the dim
Pit of oblivion swallows him.
In fame unmeasured, praise too high,
Lies danger: God's sharp lightnings fly
To stagger mountains. Then, I choose
Wealth that invites no rankling hate;
Neither to lay towns desolate,
Nor wear the chains of those who lose
Freedom and life to war and Fate.

*The sound of women's voices excitedly shouting and cheering is heard.
One or two* ELDERS *go out, and return immediately to report.
The following remarks are made severally by various members of
the* CHORUS.

Since the beacon's news was heard
Rumour flies through every street.
Ought we to believe a word?
Is it some inspired deceit?
Childish, crack-brained fantasy!
Wing your hopes with such a tale,
Soon you'll find that fire can lie,
Facts can change, and trust can fail.
Women all are hasty-headed:
Beacons blaze – belief rejoices;
All too easily persuaded.
Rumour fired by women's voices,
As we know, is quickly spread;
– As we know, is quickly dead!

*The* CHORUS *depart; and an interval representing the lapse of
several days now takes place. After the interval the* CHORUS
*re-appear in great excitement.*

CHORUS: We shall soon know whether this relay-race of
    flame,
This midnight torch-parade, this beacon-telegraph,
Told us the truth, or if the fire made fools of us –
All a delightful dream! Look! There's a herald coming
Up from the shore, wearing a crown of olive-leaves!
And, further off, a marching column of armed men,
Sheathed in hot dust, tells me this herald won't stand dumb
Or light a pinewood fire to announce the smoke of Troy!
Either his news doubles our happiness, or else –
The gods forbid all else! Good shows at first appearance,
Now may the proof be good! He who prays otherwise
For Argos – let him reap the folly of his soul!

*Enter a* HERALD.

HERALD: Argos! Dear earth my fathers trod! After ten years
    Today I have come home! All other hopes were false,
    But this proves true! I dared not think my own land would

60

In death receive me to my due and dearest rest.
Now blest be Argos, and the sun's sweet light, and Zeus,
God of this realm, and Pythian Apollo, who no more
Aims against us the shafts of his immortal bow.
You fought us, Phoebus, by Scamander long enough:
Be Saviour now, be Healer; once, not twice, our death!
Gods of the city's gathering, hear my prayer; and thou,
Hermes, dear Guardian, Herald, every herald's god;
And you, heroes of old, whose blessing sent us forth,
Bless the returning remnant that the sword has spared!
O house of kings! Beloved walls! O august thrones!
You deities who watch the rising sun, watch now!
Welcome with shining eyes the royal architect
Of towering glories to adorn his ancient throne.
To you, and every Argive citizen, Agamemnon
Brings light in darkness; come, then, greet him royally,
As fits one in whose hands Zeus the Avenger's plough
Passed over Troy, to split her towers, scar and subdue
Her fields, and from her fair soil extirpate her seed.
So harsh a halter Atreus' elder son has thrown
Around Troy's neck, and now comes home victorious
To claim supremest honours among mortal men.
For neither Paris now, nor his accomplice town,
Can boast their deed was greater than their punishment.
Found guilty of theft and robbery, he has forfeited
His treasured spoil, destroyed his father's house and throne,
And made his people pay twice over for his sin.

CHORUS: Herald of the Greek army, greeting! Welcome
    home!

HERALD: Thanks. For ten years I've prayed for life; now I
    can die.

CHORUS: Longing for Argos, for your home, tormented you?

HERALD: Cruelly; and now my cloak is wet with tears of joy.

CHORUS: Your suffering had its happy side.

HERALD:                                    What do you mean?

CHORUS: Your love and longing were returned. Is that not
   happy?

HERALD: You mean that Argos longed for us, as we for her?

CHORUS: Our hearts were dark with trouble. We missed and
   needed you.

HERALD: What caused your trouble? An enemy?

CHORUS:                                    I learnt long ago,
   *Least said is soonest mended.*

HERALD:                        But was Argos threatened
   In the king's absence?

CHORUS:                      Friend, you said just now that death
   Was dearly welcome. Our hearts echo what you felt.

HERALD: Yes, I could die, now the war's over, and all well.
   Time blurs the memory; some things one recalls as good,
   Others as hateful. We're not gods; then why expect
   To enjoy a lifetime of unbroken happiness?
   To think what we went through! If I described it all,
   The holes we camped in, dirt and weariness and sweat;
   Or out at sea, with storms all night, trying to sleep
   On a narrow board, with half a blanket; and all day,
   Miserable and sick, we suffered and put up with it.
   Then, when we landed, things were worse. We had to camp
   Close by the enemy's wall, in the wet river-meadows,
   Soaked with the dew and mist, ill from damp clothes, our
      hair
   Matted like savages'. If I described the winter, when
   In cruel snow-winds from Ida birds froze on the trees;
   Or if I told of the fierce heat, when Ocean dropped
   Waveless and windless to his noon-day bed, and slept . . .

   Well, it's no time for moaning; all that's over now.
   And those who died out there – it's over for them too;
   No need to jump to orders; they can take their rest.

Why call the roll of those who were expendable,
And make the living wince from old wounds probed again?
Nor much hurrahing either, if we're sensible.
For us who've come safe home the good weighs heaviest,
And what we've suffered counts for less. The praise that's
    due,
Proudly inscribed, will show these words to the bright sun:

*The Argive army conquered Troy,*
*And brought home over land and sea*
*These hard-won spoils, the pride and joy*
*Of ancient palaces, to be*
*Trophies of victory, and grace*
*The temples of the Hellene race.*

Let Argos hear this, and receive her general home
With thanks and praise. Let Zeus, who gave us victory,
Be blest for his great mercy. I have no more to say.

CHORUS: Well, I was wrong, I own it. Old and ready to
    learn
Is always young. But this great news is for the palace,
And chiefly Clytemnestra, whose wealth of joy we share.

    CLYTEMNESTRA *has appeared at the palace door.*

CLYTEMNESTRA: I sang for joy to hail this victory long ago,
When the first fiery midnight message told that Troy
Was sacked and shattered. Someone then took me to task:
'Beacons! So you believe them? Troy, you think, is taken?
Typical female hopefulness!' Remarks like these
Exposed my folly. Yet I made thankful sacrifice,
And throughout Argos women gathered to celebrate
Victory with songs of praise in temples of all the gods,
And feed their scented fires with rich flesh-offerings.
I have no need to hear your detailed narrative;
I'll hear all from the king's own lips. But first, to greet
Fitly and soon my honoured husband's home-coming –
For to a wife what day is sweeter than when she,

63

Receiving by God's mercy her lord safe home from war,
Flings wide the gates in welcome? – take to him this mes-
 sage:
Let him come quickly; Argos longs for him; and he
Will find at home a wife as faithful as he left,
A watch-dog at his door; knowing one loyalty;
To enemies implacable; in all ways unchanged.
No seal of his have I unsealed in these ten years.
Of pleasure found with other men, or any breath
Of scandal, I know no more than how to dip hot steel.

 *Exit* CLYTEMNESTRA *to the palace.*

HERALD: That's a strange boast – and more strange, as more
 full of truth.

Is it not scandal that a queen should speak such words?

CHORUS: Strange? No! Her style eludes you. We interpret
 her.

A very proper statement – unimpeachable!

Now, Herald, tell us of our loved King Menelaus:

Has he come? Did he sail with you? Is he safely home?

HERALD: That false good news you ask for – I can't give it
 you,

My friends; delusion would not comfort you for long.

CHORUS: Telling a fair tale falsely cannot hide the truth;

When truth and good news part, the rift shows plain enough.

HERALD: Then here it is: Menelaus has vanished, ship and all!

CHORUS: You mean, he sailed with you from Troy, and then
 a storm

Fell on the fleet, and parted his ship from the rest?

HERALD: Good marksman! An age of agony pointed in three
 words.

CHORUS: But Menelaus – what was it thought had happened
 to him?

Is he given up for lost? Or may he yet survive?

HERALD: No one can tell, for no one knows; except, perhaps,
The Sun, who fosters every earthly creature's life.

CHORUS: You mean, I think, that when this storm had
    scourged our fleet
Some anger of the heavenly powers was satisfied?
HERALD: Can it be right to foul this fair and holy day,
Blurting bad news? After our thanksgiving to the gods,
Such speech is out of place. When a man stands recounting
With bloodshot stare catastrophe and horror, an army dead,
The body of State staggered and gored, homes emptied, men
Blasted, lashed out of life by fire and sword, War's whips –
If such tales were my wares, this triumph-song of disaster
I bring, would suit well. But my news is victory,
Brought to a jubilant city – how can I countervail
Such good with sorrow, tell of the murderous armed
    alliance
Fate forged with angry gods to pursue and harass us?
For fire and water, age-old enemies, made league,
And pledged good faith in combined slaughter of Greek men.
One night a vicious swell rose with a gale from Thrace;
The sky was a mad shepherd tearing his own flock;
Ship against ship butted like rutting rams; mountains
Of wind and water leapt, surge swallowed and rain
    threshed.
At dawn, where were the ships? The bright sun beamed –
    we saw
The Aegean flowering thick with faces of dead Greeks
And scraps of wrecks . . .

                    Our hull had held, and we came through.
It was no mortal hand that gripped our helm that night:
Some god, by guile or intercession, saved our lives.
Fortune sat smiling on our prow; we sprang no leak,
Nor ran aground on rocks. In the next morning's light,
Stunned, sickened, still incredulous of our own luck,
We brooded, thinking of our maimed and battered fleet.

And they, if any still draw breath, now speak of us
As caught in the same fate we picture theirs. . . . But yet,
May best prove truest! For Menelaus, more than all else
Expect him home. If any searching shaft of sun
Sees him alive and well, by the providence of Zeus
Not yet resolved to exterminate this house – there's hope
That Menelaus will yet come safe to his own home.
And every word you have heard me speak is the plain truth.

*The* MESSENGER *goes, in the direction from which he came.*

CHORUS: Who was the unknown seer whose voice –
Uttered at venture, but instinct
With prescience of what Fate decreed –
Guessing infallibly, made choice
Of a child's name, and deftly linked
Symbol with truth, and name with deed,
Naming, inspired, the glittering bride
Of spears, for whom men killed and died,
Helen, the Spoiler? On whose lips
Was born that fit and fatal name,
To glut the sea with spoil of ships,
Spoil souls with swords, a town with flame?
The curtained softness of her bed
She left, to hear the Zephyr breathe
Gigantic in tall sails; and soon
Comes hue and cry – armed thousands fly
Tracing her trackless oar, and sheathe
Their keels in Simois' shingly bank,
Near fields where grass today grows rank
In soil by war's rich rain made red.

And anger – roused, relentless, sure –
Taught Troy that words have double edge,
That men and gods use *bond* and *pledge*
For love past limit, doom past cure:

66

Love seals the hearts of bride and groom;
And seal of love is seal of doom.
Loud rings the holy marriage-song
As kinsmen honour prince and bride;
The hour is theirs – but not for long.
Wrath, borne on Time's unhurrying tide,
Claims payment due for double wrong –
The outraged hearth, the god defied.
And songs are drowned in tears, and soon
Must Troy the old learn a new tune;
On Paris, once her praise and pride,
She calls reproach, that his proud wooing
Has won his own and her undoing:
Her sons beset on every side,
Her life-blood mercilessly spilt –
Hers is the loss, and his the guilt.

There was a shepherd once who reared at home
A lion's cub. It shared with sucking lambs
Their milk – gentle, while bone and blood were young.
The children loved it; the old watched and smiled.
Often the shepherd held it like a child
High in his arms; and often it would seek
His hand with soft eyes and caressing tongue,
Tense with the force of hunger. But in time
It showed the nature of its kind. Repaying
Its debt for food and shelter, it prepared
A feast unbidden. Soon the nauseous reek
Of torn flesh filled the house; a bloody slime
Drenched all the ground from that unholy slaying,
While helpless weeping servants stood and stared.
The whelp once reared with lambs, now grown a beast,
Fulfils his nature as Destruction's priest!

And so to Troy there came
One in whose presence shone
Beauty no thought can name:
A still enchantment of sweet summer calm;
A rarity for wealth to dote upon;
Glances whose gentle fire
Bestowed both wound and balm;
A flower to melt man's heart with wonder and desire.
But time grew ripe, and love's fulfilment ran
Aside from that sweet course where it began.
She, once their summer joy,
Transmuted, now like a swift curse descended
On every home, on every life
Whose welcome once befriended
The outlaw wife;
A fiend sent by the god of host and guest,
Whose law her lover had transgressed,
To break his heart, and break the pride of Troy.

When Earth and Time were young,
A simple ancient saw
Phrased on the common tongue
Declared that man's good fortune, once mature,
Does not die childless, but begets its heir;
That from life's goodness grows, by Nature's law,
Calamity past cure
And ultimate despair.
I think alone; my mind
Rejects this general belief.
Sin, not prosperity, engenders grief;
For impious acts breed their own kind,
And evil's nature is to multiply.
The house whose ways are just in word and deed
Still as the years go by
Sees lasting wealth and noble sons succeed.

So, by law of consequence,
Pride or Sin the Elder will,
In the man who chooses ill,
Breed a Younger Insolence.
Sin the Younger breeds again
Yet another unseen Power
Like the Powers that gave it birth:
Recklessness, whose force defies
War and violence, heaven and earth;
Whose menace like a black cloud lies
On the doomed house hour by hour,
Fatal with fear, remorse, and pain.

But Justice with her shining eyes
Lights the smoke-begrimed and mean
Dwelling; honours those who prize
Honour; searches far to find
All whose hearts and hands are clean;
Passes with averted gaze
Golden palaces which hide
Evil armed in insolence;
Power and riches close combined,
Falsely stamped with all men's praise,
Win from her no reverence.
Good and evil she will guide
To their sure end by their appointed ways.

*Enter* AGAMEMNON *in his chariot, followed by another chariot
bearing spoils of war and* CASSANDRA.

CHORUS: King! Heir of Atreus! Conqueror of Troy!
What greeting shall we bring? What shall we say
    To voice our hearts' devotion,
    Observe both truth and measure,
Be neither scant nor fulsome in our love?
Many, whose conscience is not innocent,

Attach high value to a show of praise.
 As ill-luck finds on all sides
 Eyes brimming with condolence
Where no true sting of sorrow pricks the heart,
So now some harsh embittered faces, forced
Into a seemly smile, will welcome you,
 And hide the hearts of traitors
 Beneath their feigned rejoicing.
Well, a wise shepherd knows his flock by face;
And a wise king can tell the flatterer's eye –
 Moist, unctuous, adoring –
The expressive sign of loyalty not felt.
Now this I will not hide: ten years ago
When you led Greece to war for Helen's sake
 You were set down as sailing
 Far off the course of wisdom.
We thought you wrong, misguided, when you tried
 To keep morale from sagging
 In superstitious soldiers
By offering sacrifice to stop the storm.
Those times are past; you have come victorious home;
Now from our open hearts we wish you well.
 Time and your own enquiries
 Will show, among your people,
Who has been loyal, who has played you false.

AGAMEMNON: First, Argos, and her native gods, receive
 from me
The conqueror's greeting on my safe return; for which,
As for the just revenge I wrought on Priam's Troy,
Heaven shares my glory. Supplications without end
Won Heaven's ear; Troy stood her trial; unfaltering
The immortals cast their votes into the urn of death,
Dooming Troy's walls to dust, her men to the sword's edge.
The acquitting urn saw hope alone come near, and pass,

Vanishing in each empty hand. Smoke, rising still,
Marks great Troy's fall; flames of destruction's sacrifice
Live yet; and, as they die, stirs from the settled ash
The wind-borne incense of dead wealth and luxury.

Now for this victory let our pious thanksgiving
Tell and re-tell Heaven's favour. We have made Troy pay
For her proud rape a woman's price. The Argive beast,
The lion rampant on all our shields, at dead of night
Sprang from the womb of the horse to grind that city's
    bones,
A ranked and ravening litter, that over wall and tower
Leaping, licked royal blood till lust was surfeited.

Thus to the gods I pay first my full salutation.
For your advice, I note it; I am of your mind,
And uphold your judgement. There are few whose inborn
    love
Warms without envy to a friend's prosperity.
Poison of jealousy laps the disappointed heart,
Doubling its grievance: pangs for its own losses match
With pangs for neighbours' wealth. Life and long observa-
    tion
Taught me the look of men whose loving show, examined,
Proves but a shadow's shadow: I speak of what I know.
One man, Odysseus, who set sail unwillingly –
At this hour dead or living? – he alone, once yoked,
With good will shared my burden.

                              For affairs of State,
And this feared disaffection, we will set a day
For assembly and debate among our citizens,
And take wise counsel; where disease wants remedy,
Fire or the knife shall purge this body for its good.

Now to my home, to stand at my own altar-hearth
And give Heaven my first greeting, whose protecting power
Sent forth, and brought me home again. May Victory,
My guardian hitherto, walk constant at my side!

*Enter* CLYTEMNESTRA *attended by* MAIDS *holding a*
*long drape of crimson silk.*

CLYTEMNESTRA: Elders and citizens of Argos! In your
    presence now
I will speak, unashamed, a wife's love for her husband.
With time dies diffidence. What I shall tell I learnt
Untaught, from my own long endurance, these ten years
My husband spent under the walls of Ilion.
First, that a woman should sit forlorn at home, unmanned,
Is a crying grief. Then, travellers, one on other's heels,
Dismayed the palace, each with worse news than the last.
Why, if my lord received as many wounds as Rumour,
Plying from Troy to Argos, gave him, he is a net,
All holes! Or had he died each time report repeated
News of his death – see him, a second Geryon,
Boasting his monstrous right, his thrice-spread quilt of
    earth –
A grave for each death, each body! Many times despair
At a cruel message noosed my throat in a hung cord,
Which force against my will untied.

                              These fears explain
Why our child is not here to give you fitting welcome,
Our true love's pledge, Orestes. Have no uneasiness.
He is in Phocis, a guest of Strophius your well-tried friend,
Who warned me of peril from two sources: first, the risk
Threatening your life at Troy; then, if conspiracy
Matured to popular revolt in Argos, fear
Of man's instinct to trample on his fallen lord.
Such was his reasoning – surely free from all suspicion.

For me – the springing torrents of my tears are all
Drawn dry, no drop left; and my sleepless eyes are sore
With weeping by the lamp long lit for you in vain.
In dreams, the tenuous tremors of the droning gnat
Roused me from dreadful visions of more deaths for you
Than could be compassed in the hour that slept with me.

There is no dearer sight than shelter after storm;
No escape sweeter than from siege of circumstance.
Now, after siege and storm endured, my happy heart
Welcomes my husband, faithful watch-dog of his home,
Our ship's firm anchor, towering pillar that upholds
This royal roof; as dear, as to a father's hope
His longed-for son, a spring to thirsty travellers,
Or sight of land unlooked-for to men long at sea.

Such praise I hold his due; and may Heaven's jealousy
Acquit us; our past suffering has been enough.

Now, dearest husband, come, step from your chariot.
But do not set to earth, my lord, the conquering foot
That trod down Troy. Servants, do as you have been bidden;
Make haste, carpet his way with crimson tapestries,
Spread silk before your master's feet; Justice herself
Shall lead him to a home he never hoped to see.
All other matters forethought, never lulled by sleep,
Shall order justly as the will of Heaven decrees.

*Clytemnestra's* MAIDS *spread a path of crimson cloth from the
chariot to the palace door.*

AGAMEMNON: Daughter of Leda, guardian of my house, your
    speech
Matches its theme, my absence; for both were prolonged.
Praise fitly spoken should be heard on other lips.
And do not with these soft attentions woman me,
Nor prostrate like a fawning Persian mouth at me

Your loud addresses; nor with your spread cloths invite
Envy of gods, for honours due to gods alone.
I count it dangerous, being mortal, to set foot
On rich embroidered silks. I would be reverenced
As man, not god. The praise of fame rings clear without
These frills and fancy foot-rugs; and the god's best gift
Is a mind free from folly. Call him fortunate
Whom the end of life finds harboured in tranquillity.

CLYTEMNESTRA: There is the sea – who shall exhaust the
  sea? – which teems
With purple dye costly as silver, a dark stream
For staining of fine stuffs, unceasingly renewed.
This house has store of crimson, by Heaven's grace, enough
For one outpouring; you are no king of beggary!
Had oracles prescribed it, I would have dedicated
Twenty such cloths to trampling, if by care and cost
I might ensure safe journey's end for this one life.
Now you are come to your dear home, your altar-hearth,
The tree, its root refreshed, spreads leaf to the high beams
To veil us from the dog-star's heat. Your loved return
Shines now like Spring warmth after winter; but when Zeus
From the unripe grape presses his wine, then through the
  house
Heat dies, and coolness comes, as through this royal door
Enters its lord, perfected to receive his own.

AGAMEMNON: I have said how I would enter with an easy
  mind.

CLYTEMNESTRA: Tell me – not contrary to your resolve –
  one thing.

AGAMEMNON: Be sure I shall do nothing against my resolve.

CLYTEMNESTRA: Might you have vowed to the gods, in
  danger, such an act?

AGAMEMNON: Yes, if someone with knowledge had pre-
  scribed it me.

CLYTEMNESTRA: Imagine Priam conqueror: what would he have done?

AGAMEMNON: Walked on embroidered satin, I have little doubt.

CLYTEMNESTRA: Then why humble your heart to men's censorious tongue?

AGAMEMNON: Why indeed? Yet the people's voice speaks with great power.

CLYTEMNESTRA: Greatness wins hate. Unenvied is unenviable.

AGAMEMNON: It does not suit a woman to be combative.

CLYTEMNESTRA: Yet it suits greatness also to accept defeat.

AGAMEMNON: Why, here's a battle! What would you not give to win?

CLYTEMNESTRA: Yield! You are victor: give me too my victory.

AGAMEMNON: Since you're resolved – [to an attendant] Come, kneel; untie my shoes; dismiss
These leathern slaves that smooth my path. And as I tread
This deep-sea treasure, may no watchful envious god
Glance from afar. It offends modesty, that I
Should dare with unwashed feet to soil these costly rugs,
Worth weight for weight of silver, spoiling my own house!
But let that pass.

       Take in this girl and treat her well.
God will reward from heaven a gentle conqueror.
Slavery is a yoke no one bears willingly; and she
Came to me by the army's gift, of all Troy's wealth
The chosen jewel.
Now, since I have been subdued to obedience in this matter,
Treading on purple I will go into my house.

CLYTEMNESTRA: Elelelelu! [a prolonged triumphant cry;
which the CHORUS accept as a formal celebration of the victor's

75

*return, while only* CASSANDRA *understands its true meaning.*
AGAMEMNON *walks alone along the purple path and enters the palace.*]

CLYTEMNESTRA: Zeus, Zeus, Fulfiller! Now fulfil these
    prayers of mine;
And let thy care accomplish all that is thy will!

CLYTEMNESTRA *enters the palace.* AGAMEMNON's *chariot is taken away by attendants.* CASSANDRA *remains seated in the second chariot.*

CHORUS: What is this persistent dread
    Haunting, hovering to show
    Signs to my foreboding soul,
    While unbidden and unpaid
    Throbs the prophet in my veins,
    While persuasive confidence
    That should rule the heart, and scorn
    Fantasies of cloudy dreams,
    Trembles, and resigns her throne?
    Once before, though far away,
    My heart knew the pregnant hour,
    When at Troy our sailors' shouts,
    As they coiled their sheets astern,
    Chimed with my triumphal song;
    And the fleet set sail for home.

    Then was guessing; now I see
    With these eyes the fleet returned.
    Yet my spirit knows again
    The foreboding hour; again
    Sings, by untaught instinct, that
    Sad, familiar, fatal dirge;
    Yields her kingdom in the flesh,
    Daunted with surmise, and feels
    Pang and pulse of groin and gut,

Blood in riot, brain awhirl,
Nerve and tissue taut, and knows
Truth must prick, where flesh is sore.
Yet I pray, may time and truth
Shame my fears; may prophecy
Vanish, and fulfilment fail!

When fortune flowers too lushly,
Decay, her envious neighbour,
Stands eager to invade;
Glory's brief hours are numbered,
And what has flowered must fade.
Bold in success, ambition
Sails on, where rocks lie hidden,
Strikes, and her debt is paid.
Yet, debts may be compounded:
When Thracian storm-winds threaten,
The merchant, for his silver,
With pious prayers devotes
A tithe in ample measure;
Into the sea he slings it,
And safe his vessel floats.
The house that offers to the envious Powers
Its wealthy surplus will not fail and die;
Zeus to their prayers will bounteously reply,
Bless each year's furrowed fields with sun and showers,
Bid harvests teem, and fear of famine fly.

But when, from flesh born mortal,
Man's blood on earth lies fallen,
A dark, unfading stain,
Who then by incantations
Can bid blood live again?
Zeus in pure wisdom ended

That sage's skill who summoned
Dead flesh to rise from darkness
And live a second time;
Lest murder cheaply mended
Invite men's hands to crime.
Were I not sure that always
Events and causes hold
Sequence divinely ordered,
And next by last controlled,
Speech would forestall reluctance,
Voice thoughts I dare not fathom,
And leave no fear untold.
But now my tongue mutters in darkness, sharing
The heart's distress, tormented with desire
To achieve some timely word, and still despairing;
While my dumb spirit smoulders with deep fire.

CLYTEMNESTRA *comes to the palace door.*

CLYTEMNESTRA: You too, Cassandra there, do you hear me?
    Get indoors.
    You may thank Zeus, this palace bears you no ill-will;
    You shall stand near our sovereign altar, and partake,
    With many other slaves, the cleansing ritual.
    Then leave that chariot; do not be proud. They say
    Heracles once was sold, and learnt to eat slaves' bread.
    If such misfortune falls, and there's no help for it –
    A house of long-established wealth is generous;
    Where meagre hopes reap opulence, it goes hard with
        slaves.
    Here you shall have your due – what's customary, and more.

CHORUS: It was to you she spoke. She waits. Was it not clear?
    Since you're a captive in the toils of destiny
    Obey, if you understand. Or do you choose defiance?

CLYTEMNESTRA: If she's not crazed, she will obey; unless
    she speaks

78

Some weird unheard-of tongue, like swallows twittering.

CHORUS: Come, now; her bidding is the best that's possible.
Leave sitting in that chariot; obey, go in.

CLYTEMNESTRA: I have no time to spend standing out here.
Already
Victims for sacrifice wait at the central hearth.
If you understand what I have said, come in at once;
If not, [*to an attendant*] since she's a foreigner, explain by
signs.

*An attendant makes signs to* CASSANDRA *to enter the palace.*

CHORUS: It's clear enough the girl needs an interpreter.
She has the look of some wild creature newly trapped.

CLYTEMNESTRA: Why, she is mad, hears only her own
frenzied thoughts.
Has she not left her city levelled with the ground? –
Yet has not sense enough to accept her owner's bit
Till she has frothed her rage out from a bloody mouth.
I will spend words no longer, to be thus ignored.

CLYTEMNESTRA *goes into the palace.*

CHORUS: I feel pity, not anger. Come, poor girl, step down;
Yield to this hard necessity; wear your new yoke.

CASSANDRA *steps down. She sees the statue of Apollo.*

CASSANDRA: O Apollo! Oh, oh! No, no, no, no! O Earth!
O Apollo!

CHORUS: Why name Apollo with this wail of agony?
He is no god of mourning, to be so invoked.

CASSANDRA: Oh, oh! O horror! O Earth! O Apollo, Apollo!

CHORUS: Again she utters blasphemy, to call Apollo,
Whose godhead may not stand in the same house with grief.

CASSANDRA: Apollo, Apollo! Leader of journeys, my
destroyer!
All this way you have led me, to destroy me again!

CHORUS: She is inspired to speak of her own sufferings.
The prophetic power stays with her even in slavery.

CASSANDRA: Apollo, Apollo! Leader of journeys, my
  destroyer!
Where have you led me? Oh! what fearful house is this?
CHORUS: Does not prophecy tell you this is Atreus' palace?
I tell you, then; so call it, and you will speak the truth.
CASSANDRA: No! but a house that hates
  The gods; whose very stones
Bear guilty witness to a bloody act;
  That hides within these gates
  Remnants of bodies hacked,
  And murdered children's bones!
CHORUS: This prophetess goes to it like a keen-scented
  hound;
We know the trail she follows, and it leads to blood.
CASSANDRA: To blood – I know. See there,
  The witness that they bear –
Those children weeping for their own blood shed,
  For their own tender flesh,
  That cruel, nameless dish
  From which their father fed!
CHORUS: We had all heard of your prophetic power; but this
Requires no prophecy to tell us of –
CASSANDRA:                          Ah, ah!
  Oh, shame! Conspiracy!
  A heart obsessed with hate
  And lurking to betray
  Pollutes this house anew
  With deadly injury
  Where deepest love was due!
Surprised, unarmed, how can he fight with Fate?
  And help is far away.
CHORUS: The first we understand – all Argos speaks of it;
But to this second prophecy I have no key.
CASSANDRA: Shame on her! She will stand –

Would there were room for doubt! –
To cleanse her lawful lord
From guilt of war – and then –
How can I speak the word?
This cleansing ritual
Shall serve his burial!
Despairing hands reach out,
Snared by a stronger hand!

CHORUS: Still I am baffled by her riddling utterance;
What can one make of prophecy so recondite?

CASSANDRA: There, there! O terror! What is this new sight?
A hunting-net, Death's weapon of attack!
And she who hunts is she who shared his bed.
Howl, Furies, howl, you bloody ravening pack,
Gorged with this house's blood, yet thirsting still;
The victim bleeds: come, Fiends, and drink your fill!

CHORUS: What fiends are these you call to bay at Death?
Your ghastly hymn has paled your cheek; and pale
The blood shrinks to your heart, as when men die
Sword-struck in battle, pulse and vision fail,
And life's warm colours fly;
See, how her utterance chokes her laboured breath!

CASSANDRA: Help! Look, a nightmare! What? will cow gore
bull,
The black-horned monarch? Save him, drag him away!
The treacherous water's poured, the lustral bath is full;
She holds him in a trap made like a gown –
She strikes! He crashes down!
Listen! It is treachery, treachery, I say!

CHORUS: Although I claim no special skill in oracles,
Her words, I feel, augur no good. Yet, after all,
What good news ever comes to men through oracles?
Prophets find bad news useful. Why, the primary aim
Of all their wordy wisdom is to make men gape.

CASSANDRA: O fear, and fear again!
    O pity! Not alone
    He suffers; with his pain
    Mingled I mourn my own!
    Cruel Apollo! Why,
    Why have you led me here?
    Only that I may share
    The death that he must die!

CHORUS: She is insane, poor girl, or god-possessed,
    And for herself alone she makes this wail,
    Unwearied in her tuneless song;
    As the shrill nightingale
    Unburdens her distracted breast,
    Sobbing *Itun, Itun*, remembering all her wrong.

CASSANDRA: Bitter was her ordeal;
    Yet by the kind gods' wish
    The lovely robe she wears
    Is feathered wings; and even
    The plaint she pours to heaven,
    Note answering note with tears,
    Rings sweet. But I must feel
    The parting of the flesh
    Before the whetted steel.

CHORUS: Whence come these violent miseries, god-inspired
    Yet void of meaning? Why with voice like doom
    Intone these horrors in heart-searing words?
    Who marked the oracular road
    Whose evil terms you trace?

CASSANDRA [*changing from the shrill declamation of prophecy to
    the quiet sadness of mourning*]: O Paris and his passion!
    O marriage-bed that slew
    His family and city!
    O sweet Scamander river
    Our thirsting fathers knew,

By whose loved banks I grew!
But soon the dark Cocytus
And Acheron shall echo
My prophecies, and witness
Whether my words are true.

CHORUS: Paris's marriage! This at last is clear
To any child. Yet in her muttered fear
Lies more than meets the sight:
With stunning pain, like a brute serpent's bite,
Her whispered cry crashes upon my ear.

CASSANDRA: O Ilion and her passion!
O city burnt and razed!
O fires my father kindled
To keep his towers defiant!
O blood of beasts he offered
From every herd that grazed!
Yet no propitiation
Could save her sons from dying
As I foretold they would;
And I will join my brothers,
And soon the ground will welcome
My warm and flowing blood.

CHORUS: Once more her utterance adds like to like.
Tell us, what god is he, so merciless,
Whose grievous hand can strike
Such deathly music from your mournful soul,
Arrows of prophecy whose course and goal
I seek, but cannot guess?

CASSANDRA: Then listen. Now my prophecy shall no more
peep
From under shy veils like a new-made bride, but blow
A bounding gale towards the sunrise, on whose surge
A crime more fearful than my murder shall at once
Sweep into blazing light. Without more mystery

I will instruct you; but first testify how close
I scent the trail of bloody guilt incurred long since.
Under this roof live day and night a ghastly choir
Venting their evil chant in hideous harmony;
Drunk with men's blood, boldly established here, they hold
Unbroken revel, Fiends of the blood royal, whom none
Can exorcize. Drinking they sit, and with their songs
Drive folly first to crime; the crime performed, in turn
They spew out the defiler of his brother's bed!
Do I miss? Or has my arrow found a mark you know?
Or am I 'lying prophet', 'gipsy', 'tale-spinner'?
Come, on your oath, bear witness: the foul history
Of Atreus' palace, sin for sin, is known to me!

CHORUS: The holiest oath could help but little. Yet I marvel
That you, bred overseas in a foreign tongue, unfold
Our city's past as truly as if you had been here.

CASSANDRA: Apollo, god of prophecy, gave me this office.

CHORUS: Did *he* lust for your mortal body, though a god?

CASSANDRA: Yes. Until now I was ashamed to speak of it.

CHORUS: We all are more reserved when we are prosperous.

CASSANDRA: He urged me hard, made warmest protest of his
love.

CHORUS: And did you lie together? Had you child by him?

CASSANDRA: I gave my word, and broke it – to the God of
Words.

CHORUS: Already god-possessed with the prophetic art?

CASSANDRA: I had foretold already the whole doom of Troy.

CHORUS: Surely the god was angry? Did he punish you?

CASSANDRA: After my sin, no one believed one word I spoke.

CHORUS: To us your prophecies seem all too credible.

CASSANDRA: Oh! Oh!
Horror and sin! Again the anguish of true vision –
Yes, sin and horror! – racks and ravages my brain.
Look! See them sit, there on the wall, like forms in dreams,

Children butchered like lambs by their own kindred. See,
What do they carry in their hands? O piteous sight!
It is their own flesh – limb and rib and heart they hold,
Distinct and horrible, the food their father ate!
I tell you, for this crime revenge grows hot: there lurks
In the home lair – as regent, say – a cowardly lion
Who plots against his master absent at the war;
While the Commander Lion who uprooted Troy,
Met by the fawning tongue, the bright obsequious ear,
Of the vile plotting she-hound, does not know what wounds
Venomed with hidden vengeance she prepares for him.
Female shall murder male: what kind of brazenness
Is that? What loathsome beast lends apt comparison?
A basilisk? Or Scylla's breed, living in rocks
To drown men in their ships – a raging shark of hell,
Dreaming of steel thrust at her husband's unarmed flesh?
You heard her superb bluff, that cry of triumph, raised
As if for a hard battle won, disguised as joy
At his safe home-coming? You are incredulous –
No matter – I say, no matter; what will come will come.
Soon you will see with your own eyes, and pity me,
And wish my prophecy had not been half so true.

CHORUS: Thyestes' feast of children's flesh we understand;
  Horror gives place to wonder at your true account;
  The rest outstrips our comprehension; we give up.

CASSANDRA: I say Agamemnon shall lie dead before your eyes.

CHORUS: Silence, you wretched outcast – or speak whole-
  some words!

CASSANDRA: No wholesome word can purge the poison of
  that truth.

CHORUS: None, if it is to be; but may the gods forbid!

CASSANDRA: You turn to prayer: others meanwhile prepare
  to kill.

CHORUS: What man can be the source of such polluting sin?

CASSANDRA: What man? You miss the main point of my prophecies.

CHORUS: How could such murder be contrived? This baffles me.

CASSANDRA: Yet I speak good Greek – all too good.

CHORUS:　　　　　　　　　　　　　　　　The oracles
Of Delphi are good Greek, but hard to understand.

CASSANDRA: Oh, oh! For pity, Apollo! Where can I escape?
This death you send me is impatient, merciless!
She, this lioness in human form, who when her lord
Was absent paired with a wolf, will take my wretched life.
Like one who mixes medicine for her enemies,
Now, while she whets the dagger for her husband's heart,
She vows to drug his dram with a memory of me,
And make him pledge my safe arrival – in my blood.

　　This robe – why should I wear what mocks me? Why still keep
This sceptre, these oracular garlands round my neck?
Before I die I'll make an end of you . . . and you . . .
Go, with my curse, go! Thus I pay my debt to you!
　　　　　　[trampling them on the ground]
Go, make some other woman rich in misery!
And let Apollo see, and witness what I do –
He who once saw me in these same insignia
Scorned, jeered at like some gipsy quack, by enemies
And friends alike, called starveling, beggar, conjuror,
Pitiable wretch – all this I bore; and now Apollo,
Who gave a portion of his own prescience to me,
Brings me from Ilion here to this death-reeking porch,
Where I shall never court crass unbelief again,
Where not my father's hearthstone but the slaughterer's block
Waits for me, warm already with a victim's blood.

Yet we shall not die unregarded by the gods.
A third shall come to raise our cause, a son resolved
To kill his mother, honouring his father's blood.
He, now a wandering exile, shall return to set
The apex on this tower of crime his race has built.
A great oath, sealed in sight of gods, binds him to exact
Full penance for his father's corpse stretched dead in dust.

Why then should I lament? Am I so pitiable?
I have watched Fate unfold her pattern: Troy endured
What she endured; her captor now, by Heaven's decree,
Ends thus. I have done with tears. I will endure my death.
O gates of the dark world, I greet you as I come!
Let me receive, I pray, a single mortal stroke,
Sink without spasm, feel the warm blood's gentle ebb,
Embrace death for my comfort, and so close my eyes.

CHORUS: O woman deep in wisdom as in suffering,
You have told us much. Yet, if you have true foreknowledge
Of your own death, why, like an ox for sacrifice,
Move thus towards the altar with intrepid step?

CASSANDRA: Friends, there is no escape, none – once the
hour has come.

CHORUS: Yet last to go gains longest time.

CASSANDRA:                              This is the day.
Retreat wins little.

CHORUS:              Courage and destiny in you
Are proudly matched.

CASSANDRA:              The happy never hear such praise.

CHORUS: Yet a brave death lends brightness to mortality.

CASSANDRA: O father! O my brothers! All your brightness
dead! . . .
I go. Now in the land of the defeated I
Will mourn my end and Agamemnon's. I have lived.

*She goes towards the door; then with a cry turns back.*

87

CHORUS: What is it? What do you see? What terror turns you back?

> CASSANDRA *gasps, with a sound of choking.*

CHORUS: You gasp, as if some nausea choked your very soul.

CASSANDRA: There is a smell of murder. The walls drip with blood.

CHORUS: The altar's ready. This is the smell of sacrifice.

CASSANDRA: It is most like the air that rises from a grave.

CHORUS. You mean the Syrian perfume sprinkled for the feast?

CASSANDRA: I am not like a bird scared at an empty bush,
Trembling for nothing. Wait: when you shall see my death
Atoned with death, woman for woman; when in place
Of him whom marriage cursed another man shall fall:
Then witness for me – these and all my prophecies
Were utter truth. This I request before I die.

CHORUS: To die is sad: sadder, to know death fore-ordained.

CASSANDRA: Yet one word more, a prophecy – or, if a dirge,
At least not mine alone. In this sun's light – my last –
I pray: when the sword's edge requites my captor's blood,
Then may his murderers, dying, with that debt pay too
For her they killed in chains, their unresisting prey!

Alas for human destiny! Man's happiest hours
Are pictures drawn in shadow. Then ill fortune comes,
And with two strokes the wet sponge wipes the drawing out.
And grief itself's hardly more pitiable than joy.

> *She goes into the palace.*

CHORUS: Of fortune no man tastes his fill.
While pointing envy notes his store,
And tongues extol his happiness,
Man surfeited will hunger still.
For who grows weary of success,

Or turns good fortune from his door
Bidding her trouble him no more?

Our king, whom Fortune loves to bless,
By the gods' will has taken Troy,
And honour crowns his safe return.
If now, for blood shed long ago,
In penance due his blood must flow,
And if his murderers must earn
Death upon death, and Fate stands so,
I ask, what mortal man can claim
That he alone was born to enjoy
A quiet life, and an untarnished name?

AGAMEMNON'S *voice is heard from inside the palace.*

AGAMEMNON: Help, help! I am wounded, murdered, here in the inner room!

CHORUS: Hush, listen! Who cried 'Murder'? Do you know that voice?

AGAMEMNON: Help, help again! Murder – a second, mortal blow!

CHORUS 1. That groan tells me the deed is done. It was the king.
Come, let's decide together on the safest plan.
2. This is what I advise – to send a herald round
Bidding the citizens assemble here in arms.
3. Too slow. I say we should burst in at once, and catch
Murder in the act, before the blood dries on the sword.
4. I share your feeling – that is what we ought to do,
Or something of that kind. Now is the time to act.
5. It's plain what this beginning points to: the assassins
Mean to establish a tyrannical regime.
6. Yes – while we talk and talk; but action, spurning sleep,
Tramples the gentle face of caution in the dust.
7. I can suggest no plan that might prove practical.

I say, let those who took this step propose the next.
8. I'm of the same opinion. If the king is dead,
I know no way to make him live by argument.
9. Then shall we patiently drag out our servile years
Governed by these disgraces of our royal house?
10. No, no! Intolerable! Who would not rather die? –
A milder fate than living under tyranny!
11. Wait; not too fast. What is our evidence? Those groans?
Are we to prophesy from them that the king's dead?
12. We must be certain; this excitement's premature.
Guessing and certain knowledge are two different things.

CHORUS: I find this view supported on all sides: that we
Make full enquiry what has happened to the king.

*The palace doors open, revealing* CLYTEMNESTRA. *At her feet*
AGAMEMNON *lies dead, in a silver bath, and wrapped in a*
*voluminous purple robe. On his body lies* CASSANDRA, *also*
*dead.*

CLYTEMNESTRA: I said, not long since, many things to match
      the time;
All which, that time past, without shame I here unsay.
How else, when one prepares death for an enemy
Who seems a friend – how else net round the deadly trap
High enough to forestall the victim's highest leap?
A great while I have pondered on this trial of strength.
At long last the pitched battle came, and victory:
Here where I struck I stand and see my task achieved.
Yes, this is my work, and I claim it. To prevent
Flight or resistance foiling death, I cast on him,
As one who catches fish, a vast voluminous net,
That walled him round with endless wealth of woven folds;
And then I struck him, twice. Twice he cried out and
      groaned;
And then fell limp. And as he lay I gave a third
And final blow, my thanks for prayers fulfilled, to Zeus,

90

Lord of the lower region, Saviour – of dead men!
So falling he belched forth his life; with cough and retch
There spurted from him bloody foam in a fierce jet,
And spreading, spattered me with drops of crimson rain;
While I exulted as the sown cornfield exults
Drenched with the dew of heaven when buds burst forth in
    Spring.

So stands the case, Elders of Argos. You may be
As you choose, glad or sorry; I am jubilant.
And, were it seemly over a *dead* man to pour
Thankoffering for safe journey, surely Justice here
Allows it, here demands it; so enriched a wine
Of wickedness this man stored in his house, and now
Returned, drains his own cursed cup to the last dregs.

CHORUS: The brute effrontery of your speech amazes us.
    To boast so shamelessly over your husband's corpse!

CLYTEMNESTRA: You speak as to some thoughtless woman:
    you are wrong.
    My pulse beats firm. I tell what you already know:
    Approve or censure, as you will; all's one to me.
    This is my husband, Agamemnon, now stone dead;
    His death the work of my right hand, whose craftsmanship
    Justice acknowledges. There lies the simple truth.

CHORUS: Vile woman! What unnatural food or drink,
    Malignant root, brine from the restless sea,
    Transformed you, that your nature did not shrink
    From foulest guilt? Argos will execrate
    Your nameless murder with one voice of hate,
    Revoke your portion with the just and free,
    And drive you outlawed from our Argive gate.

CLYTEMNESTRA: Yes! Now you righteously mulct *me* with
    banishment,
    Award me public curses, roars of civic hate.

Why, once before, did you not dare oppose this man?
Who with as slight compunction as men butcher sheep,
When his own fields were white with flocks, must sacrifice
His child, and my own darling, whom my pain brought
     forth –
He killed her for a charm to stop the Thracian wind!
He was the one you should have driven from Argos; he,
Marked with his daughter's blood, was ripe for punishment.
But *my* act shocks your ears, whets your judicial wrath!
Your threats doubtless rely on force – you have your men
And weapons: try your strength in fair fight against mine.
Win, and you may command me. If – please Heaven – you
     lose,
Old as you are, you shall be taught some wisdom yet.
CHORUS: Such boasts show folly in a crafty mind.
     So surely as your robe blazons your crime
     In those red drops, shall your own head bow low
     Under a bloody stroke. Wait but the time:
     Friendless, dishonoured, outcast, you shall find
     Your debt fall due, and suffer blow for blow.
CLYTEMNESTRA: Is it so? Then you shall hear the righteous
     oath I swear.
By Justice, guardian of my child, now perfected;
By her avenging Fury, at whose feet I poured
His blood: I have no fear that *his* avenger's tread
Shall shake this house, while my staunch ally now as then,
Aegisthus, kindles on my hearth the ancestral fire.
With such a shield, strength marches boldly on. Meanwhile,
He who was sweet to every Trojan Chryseis,
And soured my life, lies here; with him his prisoner,
His faithful soothsayer, who shared his berth, and knew
Sailors' lasciviousness; their ends both richly earned.
He – as you see him; she first, like the dying swan,
Sang her death-song, and now lies in her lover's clasp.

Brought as a variant to the pleasures of my bed,
She lends an added relish now to victory.

CHORUS: Come, look on him, and weep.
O that some merciful swift fate,
Not wasting-sick nor wry with pain,
Would bid me share his ever-endless sleep!
Low lies the kindly guardian of our State,
Who fought ten years to win
Redress for woman's sin;
Now by a woman slain.

Helen! Infatuate Helen! You who spilt
Beneath Troy's wall lives without number! You
Now on your house have fixed a lasting guilt
Which every age will tell anew.
Surely, that day you fled beyond recall,
A curse of grief already grew
Deep-rooted in this royal hall.

CLYTEMNESTRA: Is fact so gross a burden?
Put up no prayers for death;
Nor turn your spleen on Helen,
As if her act had ordered
The fate of fighting thousands
And robbed their souls of breath;
Or from her fault alone
Such cureless grief had grown.

CHORUS: Spirit of hate, whose strong curse weighs
Hard on the house and heirs of Tantalus,
Your power it is engenders thus
In woman's brain such evil art,
And darkens all my bitter days.
It is your hateful form I see rejoice,
Standing like crow on carrion; your voice
Whose execrable song affronts both ear and heart.

CLYTEMNESTRA : You now speak more in wisdom,
    Naming the thrice-gorged Fury
    That hates and haunts our race.
    Hers is the thirst of slaughter,
    Still slaked with feud and vengeance,
    Till, with each wrong requited,
    A new thirst takes its place.

CHORUS : This grievous power whose wrath you celebrate
    With cursed truth, no royal house's fall,
    No mad catastrophe, can ever sate.
    O piteous mystery! Is Zeus not lord?
    Zeus, Zeus, alas! doer and source of all?
    Could even this horror be, without his sovereign word?

    Sad, silent king! How shall I mourn your death?
    How find the heart's true word, to prove me friend?
    Here where you spent your dying breath,
    Caught by the ruthless falsehood of a wife,
    In the foul spider's web fast bound you lie.
    Unholy rest, and most ignoble end –
    That man like beast should die
    Pierced with a two-edged knife!

CLYTEMNESTRA : This murder's mine, you clamour.
    I was his wife; but henceforth
    My name from his be freed!
    Dressed in my form, a phantom
    Of vengeance, old and bitter,
    On that obscene host, Atreus,
    For his abhorrent deed,
    Has poured this blood in payment,
    That here on Justice' altar
    A man for babes should bleed.

CHORUS : And are you guiltless? Some revengeful Power
    Stood, maybe, at your side; but of this blood

Who will, who could absolve you? Hour by hour
On his unyielding course the black-robed King,
Pressing to slaughter, swells the endless flood
Of crimson life by pride and hate released
From brothers' veins – till the due reckoning,
When the dried gore shall melt, and Ares bring
Justice at last for that unnatural feast.

Sad, silent king! How shall I mourn your death?
How find the heart's true word, to prove me friend?
Here where you spent your dying breath,
Caught by the ruthless falsehood of a wife,
In the foul spider's web fast bound you lie.
Unholy rest, and most ignoble end –
That man like beast should die
Pierced with a two-edged knife!

CLYTEMNESTRA: The guile I used to kill him
He used himself the first,
When he by guile uprooted
The tender plant he gave me,
And made this house accurst.
When on my virgin daughter
His savage sword descended,
My tears in rivers ran;
If now by savage sword-thrust
His ageing days are ended,
Let shame and conscience ban
His boasts, where he pays forfeit
For wrong his guile began.

CHORUS: Where, where lies Right? Reason despairs her
        powers,
Mind numbly gropes, her quick resources spent.
Our throne endangered, and disaster near,
Where can I turn? I fear

Thunder that cracks foundations, blood-red showers;
The light rain slacks – the deluge is in store.
Justice, in harmony with Fate's intent,
Hardens her hold to shake the earth once more.

O earth, O earth! Would that some timely chance
Had laid me in your lap, before my eyes
Had seen him laid so low,
Lord of this silver-walled inheritance!
Who will inter him? Who lament the dead?
Will *you* wear mourning for disguise?
Bewail the husband whom your own hand killed?
For his high glories offer gifts of lies?
Since Justice answers, No!
By whom shall tears of honest love be shed,
His graveside ritual of praise fulfilled?

CLYTEMNESTRA: That question's not your business.
I felled him; I despatched him;
And I will earth his bones.
No troops from house or city
Shall beat their breasts and lay him
In vaults of bronze and marble
With seemly civic groans.
But, as is fit, his daughter
Shall meet him near the porchway
Of those who perished young;
His loved Iphigenia
With loving arms shall greet him,
And gagged and silent tongue.

CHORUS: Reproach answers reproach; truth darkens still.
She strikes the striker; he who dared to kill
Pays the full forfeit. While Zeus holds his throne,
This maxim holds on earth: *the sinner dies*.
That is God's law. Oh, who can exorcize

This breeding curse, this canker that has grown
Into these walls, to plague them at its will?

CLYTEMNESTRA: *The sinner dies*: you have reached the truth
    at last.
Now to the Powers that persecute
Our race I offer a sworn pact:
With this harsh deed and bitter fact
*I* am content; let *them* forget the past,
Leave us for ever, and oppress
Some other house with murderous wickedness.
I ask no weight of wealth;
For me it will suffice
To purchase, at this price,
For our long sickness, health.

             *Enter* AEGISTHUS.

AEGISTHUS: O happy day, when Justice comes into her own!
Now I believe that gods, who dwell above the earth,
See what men suffer, and award a recompense:
Here, tangled in a net the avenging Furies wove,
He lies, a sight to warm my heart; and pays his blood
In full atonement for his father's treacherous crime.

Here is the story plain. There was dispute between
Atreus, Agamemnon's father, who ruled Argos then,
And my father Thyestes, his own brother; whom
Atreus drove out from home and city. He came back;
Sat as a piteous suppliant at Atreus' hearth;
Gained his request – in part: his own blood did not stain
His childhood's home. But Atreus, this man's father, gave
His guest, my father, a host's gift; a gift more full
Of eagerness than love. He feigned a feasting-day,
And amidst lavish meats served him his own sons' flesh.
The feet and the splayed fingers he concealed, putting
The other parts, unrecognizably chopped small,

Above them. Each guest had his table; and this dish
Was set before my father. He, in ignorance,
At once took that which prompted no close scrutiny,
And tasted food from which, as you now see, our house
Has not recovered. Then he recognized, in all
Its loathsomeness, what had been done. With one deep
   groan,
Back from his chair, vomiting murdered flesh, he fell;
Cursed Pelops' race with an inexorable curse;
With his foot sent the table crashing wide, and screamed,
'So crash to ruin the whole house of Tantalus!'

   That deed gave birth to what you now see here, this death.
I planned his killing, as was just: I was the third
Child of Thyestes, then a brat in baby-clothes;
Spared, and sent off with my distracted father, till,
Full-grown, Justice restored me to my native land.
I, from a distance, plotted this whole evil snare,
And caught my man. Thus satisfied, I could die now,
Seeing Agamemnon in the trap of Justice, dead.
CHORUS: Aegisthus, we acquit you of insults to the dead.
   But since you claim that you alone laid the whole plot,
   And thus, though absent, took his blood upon your hands,
   I tell you plainly, your own life is forfeited;
   Justice will curse you, Argive hands will stone you dead.
AEGISTHUS: So, this is how you lecture, from the lower deck,
   The master on the bridge? Then you shall learn, though old,
   How harsh a thing is discipline, when reverend years
   Lack wisdom. Chains and the distress of hunger are
   A magic medicine, of great power to school the mind.
   Does not this sight bid you reflect? Then do not kick
   Against the goad, lest you should stumble, and be hurt.
CHORUS: You woman! While he went to fight, you stayed at
   home;

Seduced his wife meanwhile; and then, against a man
Who led an army, *you* could scheme this murder! Pah!
AEGISTHUS: You still use words that have in them the seed of
    tears.
Your voice is most unlike the voice of Orpheus: he
Bound all who heard him with delight; your childish
    yelps
Annoy us, and will fasten bonds on you yourselves.
With hard control you will prove more amenable.
CHORUS: Control! Are we to see *you* king of Argos – you,
Who, after plotting the king's murder, did not dare
To lift the sword yourself?
AEGISTHUS:                    To lure him to the trap
Was plainly woman's work; I, an old enemy,
Was suspect. Now, helped by his wealth, I will attempt
To rule in Argos. The refractory shall not
Be fed fat like show-horses, but shall feel the yoke –
A heavy one. Hunger and darkness joined will soon
Soften resistance.
CHORUS:            Then, if you're so bold, why not
Yourself with your own hands plunder your enemy?
Instead, a woman, whose life makes this earth unclean
And flouts the gods of Argos, helped you murder him!
Oh, does Orestes live? Kind Fortune, bring him home,
To set against these two his sword invincible!
AEGISTHUS: Then, since your treason's militant, you shall
    soon learn
That it is foolish to insult authority.
Ready, there! Forward, guards! [*Armed soldiers rush in.*]
                    Here's work for you. Each man
Handle his sword.
CHORUS:          Our swords are ready. We can die.
AEGISTHUS: 'Die'! We accept the omen. Fortune hold the
    stakes!

CLYTEMNESTRA: Stop, stop, Aegisthus, dearest! No more
    violence!
  When this first harvest ripens we'll reap grief enough.
  Crime and despair are fed to bursting; let us not
  Plunge deeper still in blood. Elders, I beg of you,
  Yield in good time to Destiny; go home, before
  You come to harm; what we have done was fore-ordained.
  If our long agony finds here fulfilment, we,
  Twice gored by Fate's long talons, welcome it. I speak
  With woman's wisdom, if you choose to understand.

AEGISTHUS: Then are these gross-tongued men to aim their
    pointed gibes
  At random, and bluff out the fate they've richly earned?

CHORUS: You'll find no Argive grovel at a blackguard's feet.

AEGISTHUS: Enough! Some later day I'll settle scores with
    you.

CHORUS: Not if Fate sets Orestes on the Argos road.

AEGISTHUS: For men in exile hopes are meat and drink; I
    know.

CHORUS: Rule on, grow fat defiling Justice – while you can.

AEGISTHUS: You are a fool; in time you'll pay me for those
    words.

CHORUS: Brag blindly on – a cock that struts before his hen!

*During these last lines the* CHORUS *have gone out two by two, the*
*last man vanishing with the last insult, leaving* CLYTEMNESTRA
*and* AEGISTHUS *alone.*

CLYTEMNESTRA: Pay no heed to this currish howling. You
    and I,
  Joint rulers, will enforce due reverence for our throne.

# THE CHOEPHORI
## OR THE LIBATION-BEARERS

# THE CHOEPHORI
## OR THE LIBATION-BEARERS

*

### CHARACTERS:

ORESTES, *son of Agamemnon, king of Argos*
PYLADES, *his friend*
CHORUS *of female servants of Clytemnestra*
ELECTRA, *daughter of Agamemnon*
A MALE SERVANT *of Clytemnestra*
CLYTEMNESTRA, *widow of Agamemnon*
NURSE OF ORESTES
AEGISTHUS, *Clytemnestra's paramour*
A MALE SERVANT *of Aegisthus*

*

*The grave of Agamemnon, outside the walls of Argos, is a low mound of earth, near which stands a primitive figure of Hermes.* ORESTES *stands by the mound;* PYLADES *a little way off. It is early morning.*

ORESTES: Hermes, Guide of dead men's souls below the earth,
Son of Zeus the Deliverer, fill your father's office:
Be my deliverer. Receive my prayer; fight in my cause.
An exile newly returned to this my land, my home,
I seek my native right. Over this mound, his tomb,
Before my deed is in hand, I call on my dead father
To hear, to sanction. [*He holds out two locks of hair.*]
Hair of my head, two locks I offer. This to Inachus,
River of home, who nursed my childhood; now I am a man,
My thanks! . . . This for my grief, my loss, and tears too late.

I was not there, dear father, to mourn your murdered body
Or stretch the farewell hand as you went lifeless forth.

Who is coming? What is this? Women in long black
cloaks –
What can it mean? More death? Fresh tears to torment our
house?
Or is my first thought true, that this procession comes
Bearing libations for my father's grave, to appease
The powers of earth? Yes, it is that and nothing else!
And yes – surely – I see my sister – it is Electra!
Electra, wrapped deeper than all the rest in sorrow!

Great Zeus, O grant me vengeance for my father's death;
Be gracious to me; fight on my side! . . . Come, Pylades,
I want to listen to these women, and learn why
They undertake this suppliant rite. Come, we'll retire.

ORESTES and PYLADES *step into shadow at one side of the stage
as* ELECTRA *and the* CHORUS *enter, carrying bowls and urns
which they set down before the grave.*

CHORUS: Bidden we come with offerings to the dead,
    With mournful, solemn tread;
    Yet not in outward grief we beat the head,
    Not with pretended pain
    The cheek by nails fresh-furrowed glistens red
    (New sign of old grief that my tortured brain
    For years has fed on); no cold careless show
    Has torn this woven robe, to feign
    Anguish in this bared breast
    Bruised for a loss whose blow
    Leaves life no laughter, pain no rest.

Through the hushed midnight house a voice rang clear;
    And hair stood stiff with fear

As anger burst from sleep, and every ear
Knew that prophetic tone
Which warns in dreams, and calls this house to hear.
From an inner room, where women sleep, that groan
Spoke like a Fate. And men who pledge their skill
To interpret visions, said
(Inspired by Heaven's will),
'Hot indignation lives among the dead,
And vengeance waits for those who kill.'

So we are sent, by her whom the gods hate,
Here to propitiate
You, Mother Earth! to avert the stroke of Fate
With pious blasphemy,
With Clytemnestra's prayer!
I fear to breathe such breath into this air.
What rite can sanctify
The ground where blood lies spilt?
O house of suffering!
Shameful and strange decline
To darkness which repels the sun, dark guilt
Which man abhors, remembering
What murders marked your royal line!

Time was, when one creed ruled the people's mind:
Reverence for royal power
Unquestioned, firm as love could bind.
Now reverence has resigned
Her faith; fear has his hour.
Success is now men's god, men's more than
    god.
Yet, though the sinner cower
Long years in the half-light,
Or flout time's vengeance safe in total night;

Yet when the scale turns Justice holds the rod,
And Fate flies swift to find
And crush the open enemies of Right.

Where earth, man's patient nurse,
Has drunk and drunk again
Man's blood, and grieving sees
The thick unmelted stain
Which pleads for vengeance, there the relentless curse
Waits unforgetful for the guilty soul
To teem with foul disease
That nothing can make whole.

As virtue's door unsealed
Is never sealed again,
So, though all streams should yield
Their purity to swell one cleansing flood,
Their force must fail, their power to purge be vain
For hands that bear the stain
Of unrequited blood.

But I, since Heaven's will gave
My town to plunder and my life to chains,
Far from my father's home am kept a slave.
So, as necessity ordains,
In duty I approve just and unjust,
Obey because I must,
And, as I can, control
The bitter hatred of my soul;
While in my cloak I hide
Tears for the rule of wrong, sin justified;
My heart held rigid with unspoken pains.

ELECTRA: Women, you who both serve and order the royal
house,

Since you have come with me to perform this rite of prayer,
Advise me. What can I say? Look at these pious gifts:
Offered with them, what prayer could please? What phrase
    or form
Honour my father's grave? Shall I say, I bring this wine,
A gift from your wife, my mother, in pledge of mutual love?
I am not brazen enough. Still less can I find fit words
To bless the pouring of holy oil on my father's earth.
The customary 'Send your blessing on those who have sent
    these wreaths'?
– And pay their crimes to the full! Or, in dishonoured
    silence,
As his blood flowed, shall I throw this drink to the thirsty
    ground
And go, like one who has cast an abomination forth,
Hurling the vessel from me, and not looking back again?
Friends, share my decision, as at home you share the hate
That rules our lives. Do not be secret; speak your mind
Without fear of – those we fear. Our fate is known to the
    gods,
And, slave or free, neither you nor I can choose or escape.
If you have better counsel to give, let me hear it now.
CHORUS: By your father's tomb, as sacred to me as an altar of
    God,
Since you command, I will speak the thought of my inmost
    heart.
ELECTRA: Then speak, and this grave shall witness.
CHORUS:                          Utter a solemn prayer,
As you pour the wine, for those who are loyal –
ELECTRA:                          Whom do you mean?
Are any loyal?
CHORUS:   Yourself; and all who hate Aegisthus.
ELECTRA: For myself, then, and for you I shall make this
    prayer?

CHORUS:                                        You know
The truth, and you can judge your course.
ELECTRA:                                        What other ally
Stands on our side?
CHORUS:                    Name in your prayer Orestes too,
Though he is far away.
ELECTRA:                    Yes, a good thought; I will.
CHORUS: Next, for the murderers: pray –
ELECTRA:                                        What shall I pray for them?
Tell me; I cannot think.
CHORUS:                    – that justice of god or man
May find them out –
ELECTRA:                    May judge, condemn – or take revenge?
CHORUS: Pray simply, 'Let one come to shed blood for blood
   shed.'
ELECTRA: Would not a prayer like that seem impious to the
   gods?
CHORUS: Why? Evil for evil is no impiety.
ELECTRA: Hermes, herald of gods, guide of the world below,
Supreme mediator, help! Speak in my cause, and bid
The powers of the deep earth, who guard our inheritance,
And Earth herself, who bears and fosters all living things
And receives from men libation to quicken her seed anew –
Bid them receive my prayers! Now for the dead I pour
Water of purification, and call his spirit: Father!
Take pity on me and on Orestes your own son.
How shall we two possess our home? We are homeless both,
Sold by our mother – her price Aegisthus, who murdered
   you.
I live like a slave; Orestes, banished, disinherited;
They, arrogant, vicious, glitter in the wealth you won.
Father, let some good chance bring Orestes here! Oh, listen,
Answer my prayer!

                    For myself, a pure heart and clean hands,

And ways and thoughts unlike my mother's, are my request.
So much for us. Next, for our enemies: let your avenger,
Father, appear; let those who killed taste death for death,
Justly! This hope I stake against my enemies' hope,
My curse to match their curse, wickedness for wickedness.
But to us, be gracious; send from the depths the blessing we
    ask,
In the name of the gods, and of the earth, and of the victory
    of right.
Such are the prayers with which I pour these offerings out;
Garland them duly with a ringing dirge, a paean for the dead.

CHORUS: Let tears toll for the dead,
    Waste for waste and loss for loss;
    Now as the wine is poured
    To avert the evil day,
    To shield the faithful head,
    And hold the curse of blood at bay,
    Let tears toll for the dead,
    And loud lament reply;
    Tears for our lost lord.
    Answer the prayer we bring;
    Hear from bewildered hearts our cry,
    Agamemnon, sacred king!

    O for a man of strength,
    A lover of deeds of war,
    Who with avenging spear
    Or bow drawn to the body's length
    Will arm himself and appear,
    A saviour to untie
    The binding curse of guilt,
    To pay the ancient score,
    Redeem this house, defy
    The murderers edge to edge and hilt to hilt!

ELECTRA: The earth has drunk the wine, my father has our
    offerings.

    But listen – here is news! [*In great excitement she picks up*
    ORESTES' *lock of hair.*]

CHORUS:                              What is it? I throb with fear.

ELECTRA: A lock of hair, cut off and laid here as a gift.

CHORUS: Whose hair? A man's? A young ripe girl's?

ELECTRA:                              Can you not tell?
    Look, it is plain!

CHORUS:          You are young, we old; instruct us, please.

ELECTRA: None of his kin but I would make such an offering.

CHORUS: One other owed this duty – she who murdered
    him.

ELECTRA: Yet – look! Colour, form, texture, all the same –

CHORUS:                              As what?
    What do you mean?

ELECTRA:              As ours, our family's; like my own!

CHORUS: But – could it be Orestes' gift, laid there by stealth?

ELECTRA: This hair is most like his.

CHORUS:                              How could he dare to come?

ELECTRA: He has sent this lock as a gift of mourning for our
    father.

CHORUS: Sent? Does it mean, Orestes never again can dare
    To tread his native earth? That moves my tears no less.

ELECTRA: Tears? No! A raging sea of gall batters *my* heart;
    The iron goes through my soul; out of the savage flood
    That surges here [*with her hands on her heart*], two thirsty drops
    I could not hold
    Fall from my eyes at sight of this dear lock of hair.
    I am right! What subject head could claim this royal tress?
    The murderess never cut this from her head – my mother,
    She, the mocker of gods, blasphemer of motherhood!
    Yet to commit my heart to this belief, that Orestes,
    Dearer than all the world, has sent this gift to our father –

No, it is hope that flatters me. Could this hair but speak
Some loving message, to end my torn heart's wavering,
And give one clear command, to trample it in the dust
If Clytemnestra cut it from her hated head;
Or, if my brother's, join my sad ritual, and bring
Grace to this tomb and honour to Agamemnon's name!
The gods we cry to know what storms toss and torment
Our journey of life; yet, if deliverance lies ahead –
*A great tree might yet grow out of a little seed.*

But look! These marks – they are footprints! Here is a
    second proof
Fitting the first – they are shaped like mine! And others
    here,
Two sets of prints, his own and some companion's. Look!
The heels, the tendons clearly outlined – their measurements
Show the same form, the same proportions, as my own.
My heart throbs painfully, my thought staggers and dies.

ORESTES *and* PYLADES *come forward.*

ORESTES: Make it your boast henceforth that when you en-
    treat the gods
To answer prayers, success is yours.

ELECTRA:                                  What do you mean?
    For what present success have I to thank the gods?

ORESTES: The prayers of years are now fulfilled before your
    eyes.

ELECTRA: Do you know my secrets? Well, what name was in
    my heart?

ORESTES: I know your heart bursts with one thought –
    Orestes' name.

ELECTRA: What then? What answer is there for me?

ORESTES:                                          Here I stand.
    Look for no nearer kin.

ELECTRA:                    This is some snare to trap me.

ORESTES: If so, I am laying a snare to trap myself.

ELECTRA:                                    You choose
  To mock my misery –
ORESTES:            – And mine: my sorrow and yours are one.
ELECTRA: Must I, then – can I call you Orestes? Is it true?
ORESTES: How slow to know me, when you see my very self!
  Yet, when you saw this lock laid as a son's offering,
  Your heart took wings, you felt you were looking into my
    face;
  You traced my footprints, found their form tally with yours,
  And knew me for your brother! Hold this hair to my head,
  Here, where it was cut. Or see this cloth here, woven
  By your hand, on your loom. Look – it is your hunting-
    scene!

      *ELECTRA looks at ORESTES in joyful assurance.*
        *He grasps her hand with a warning gesture.*

  Steady! You must not let this joy undo your caution.
  I know our nearest kin are our worst enemies.
CHORUS: Dear prince, precious possession of your father's
    house,
  Living hope of salvation, watered with our tears,
  Now your stout heart must win you back your father's right.
ELECTRA: Dear, dearest face! You are four joys in one to me.
  For I must call you father; and all the love I owe
  My mother, whom I justly hate, is yours as well;
  My sister Iphigenia, cruelly killed – her share
  Of love I give you; last, you are my faithful brother;
  Your name alone has saved my life here from dishonour.
  May Victory, Right, and Zeus supreme stand at your side!
ORESTES: Zeus, Zeus! Behold us, and the deed we undertake.
  Behold the eagle's brood bereaved; the eagle killed,
  Caught in a net of death, in a cruel viper's coils.
  Behold lean hunger tyrannize their helplessness;
  Their strength half-fledged, daring to claim their father's
    spoils.

Even so, Zeus, look now on Electra and on me,
Orphans and exiles both. Our father honoured you
With prayer and countless offerings: if you take our lives,
Where will you find a hand so liberal in sacrifice?
Let the eagle's brood but perish – where are your messen-
 gers
To blazon to men's eyes your mystic certainties?
Blast with your wrath this regal stock – what pious hand
Shall grace your shrines with offerings? Then save our house;
Raise strength from utter weakness, glory from the grave!
CHORUS: O children, saviours of your father's hearth, speak
 low!
Someone may overhear, and for mere love of talk
Blab to our rulers, whom God grant me yet to see
Dead, and their flesh vanish in spitting pitch and flame!
ORESTES: The word of Apollo is of great power and cannot
 fail.
His voice, urgent, insistent, drives me to dare this peril,
Chilling my heart's hot blood with recital of threatened
 terrors,
If I should fail to exact fit vengeance, like for like,
From those who killed my father. This was the god's com-
 mand:
'Shed blood for blood, your face set like a flint. The price
They owe no wealth can weigh.' My very life, he said,
Would pay, in endless torment, for disobedience.
First he revealed what things men must perform, to soothe
Anger of spirits of earth; then, if such anger rise,
What plagues break forth: the spreading scab whose rabid
 teeth
Eat at the flesh till human shape is gone; the white
Fungus that flowers upon the scab. But when, he said,
A father's blood lies unavenged, and time grows ripe,
The neglectful son sees yet more fearful visitations,

As, towards eyes that strain and peer in darkness, come
The attacking Furies, roused by inherited blood-guilt,
Armed with arrows of the dark, with madness, false night-
        terrors,
To harass, plague, torment – to scourge him forth from his
        city
With the brazen lash, in loathed and abject filthiness.
Banquet and wine, grace of libation, he may not share –
This was the oracle's word; his father's anger, unseen,
Bars him from every altar; no man may receive him
Or share his lodging; scorned, friendless and alone, at
        length
He lies a shrivelled husk, horribly embalmed by death.

May I put my trust in oracles like these? or not?
Even if I cannot trust them, yet I must do this deed.
To this one end my will is urged by many motives:
The god's command, grief for my father; and with these
Loss of my patrimony, shame that my proud citizens,
Glorious in every land for the courage that conquered Troy,
Live thus enslaved to a woman – no, to a pair of women!
Aegisthus! Woman or man, he shall learn his lesson now.

ORESTES *and* ELECTRA *stand on either side of the tomb, and with
the* CHORUS *begin a formal lament, and invocation of the spirit
of Agamemnon.*

CHORUS: Hear now, you powerful Fates!
        Receive our prayer, and send
        By Zeus our Father's hands
        Fulfilment of that end
        Which fervent hope awaits
        And our just cause demands.

        Justice exacts her debt;
        The voice of Justice cries:

Let word pay word, let hatred get
Hatred in turn, let murderous blow
Meet blow that murdered; for the prize
Of sin is death; of pride, to be controlled.
A law three ages old
Tells man this must be so.

ORESTES: Father, father of sorrows, O can I,
Severed from you as far as pole from pole,
Still by some loving speech or timely deed
Send a fair wind of comfort to your soul,
A light to cheer the dark bed where you lie
Held for eternity?
And when your suppliant children, last descent
Of Atreus, pay their due
Of praise and fond lament,
Can you, though dead, yet heed
Their offering, and know their love is true?

CHORUS: My child, a dead man's spirit is not tamed
By fire's fierce jaws; his anger still will rise.
The dead is mourned; the murderer brought to light;
When with hot zeal, passion of children's tears,
A father's name is named,
Both word and act of mourning exercise
Justice, pursue and harass left and right
The guilty soul with searching fears.

ELECTRA: Then, father, hear our tears' alternate song.
Look on us, each your child,
Crying our grief to wake your tomb –
This earth twice burdened with our double wrong –
Both suppliants, both exiled.
Where is one single good, not rendered vain
By universal pain?
What hope have we to wrestle with our doom?

CHORUS: Yet from these groaning wrongs

May rise, if Heaven will,
Voices of hope more fair;
Our graveside dirge may still
Give place to triumph-songs;
The royal banquet-room
Shall flow with wine to pledge the royal heir
And bid him welcome home.

ORESTES: Would you had died under the Trojan wall,
My father, pierced with Lycian sword or spear,
Leaving your house enriched, your fame her boast,
Your children honoured by the eyes of all
In Argive streets; while on that foreign coast,
Your tomb, homage of countless hands, should rear
Its far-seen, stately height,
And glory should make light
The loss whose shame touches your house so near.

CHORUS: Like a new star in subterranean gloom,
Welcomed as friend by those who nobly died,
You should have reigned, a king revered by kings,
Close to the throne which rules supreme the wide
Realms under earth; for your word once could sway
Monarchs whose hand held power of grace or doom,
Whose sceptre none dared disobey.

ELECTRA: Why wish for that? Why should our father lie
Buried beside Scamander, one sad mound
Among the host of those who went to die
Under the Trojan wall? Could not, instead,
The murderers, in nature's course, have found
Before their fatal act,
Some casual end? and we, unracked
By anguish, hear from far that they were dead?

CHORUS: A golden wish! Too great,
Daughter, for Heaven to grant
To those of mortal state;

For thought is free. – And yet,
Courage! The double chant
Of your reverberant hands
Performs its spell; the powers
Of earth arm in your cause;
The loathed oppressor stands
Guilty of broken laws;
The children claim their debt,
And cry, 'The fight is ours!'

ORESTES: Zeus of the lower earth,
Zeus, sender of vengeance late but strong
Up from the depth of hell
To crush the doer of reckless wrong,
Has our cry performed its spell?
Has it pierced like an arrow through
To the hidden heart of earth?
Shall like to like give birth,
Father to son, and deed to vengeance due?

CHORUS: May the moment come when I
Over the slaughtered wife,
Over her stricken mate,
Raise the triumphant sacramental cry!
Why should I hide the hate
Which in my heart is rife,
If the hope that wings my thought is heaven-sent,
A tempest savage and high
Of passion on vengeance bent?

ELECTRA: I tremble with new despair;
Surely the hand of Zeus could never fall
To shatter their guilty heads,
Since fathers' and mothers' right is in his care?
Would Zeus but strike, lay bare
His judgement in the eyes of all!
Listen to me,

You Powers of earth and night,
Let wrong give place to right!
That is my just and only plea.
CHORUS: Courage! The gods ordain
That blood by murder shed
Cries from the ground for blood to flow again.
The Furies, sent by anger of the dead,
Howl for destruction, pain on pain,
Ruin to bring fresh ruin in its train.
ORESTES: When will you hear, thrones of the world below?
Strong Curses of the dead, see our disgrace;
See the last remnants of the Atreid race
Exiled and helpless. Zeus, where can we go?
CHORUS: Hearing your voice thus bitter with despair,
My own heart throbs foreboding, and fresh fear
At each word darkens hope; but when again
The light of confidence shines clear
Your courage calms my pain,
Till all grows bright and fair.
ELECTRA: What shall we speak to rouse the angry dead?
What but the wrongs our mother made us bear?
Fawn on us as she may,
Let her beware!
For such wrongs are not smoothed away.
The savage cubs the she-wolf bred
Are like their mother: fawn on them who dare!
CHORUS: Like an Oriental mourner
Beating the breast and head,
Like a Persian wailing-woman
I mourned for Agamemnon
When he lay dead.
Then fast the strokes descended
From fingers clenched for bruising
And arms for strength extended,

> And loud with blows resounded
> My bruised and piteous head.

ELECTRA: O fierce, flint-hearted mother!
> To a flinty grave you bore him;
> A king, by no procession
> Through mourning streets attended;
> A husband, laid unhonoured,
> Unwept in a cruel bed.

ORESTES: Not alone on king and husband
> This deep dishonour lay;
> But a father was dishonoured;
> And by the grace of Heaven,
> And by my own hands' doing,
> She for this too shall pay;
> And when her life is ended
> Let mine be cast away.

CHORUS: This further you must know:
> His flesh was mutilated;
> And she who earthed him so
> Did what she did with purpose
> To make his blood a burden
> To bow your life and crush you
> With thought of him so hated,
> And in such shame laid low.

ELECTRA: And so my father perished;
> And I, despised, unwanted,
> Shoved to one side, and shunned
> Like an ulcerous dog, let flow
> Tears reckless and unstinted
> As laughter, sobbing unseen.
> Let this on your heart be printed
> When you hear what grief can mean.

CHORUS: Let the horrors we have told you
> Pierce with a clear cry

Through to your heart, and hold you
To a firm and settled will.
The past no man can alter;
What Fate holds secret still
Let your courage burn to try.
For none can deny your right
If you stand to fight
With a strength that will not falter.

ORESTES: Father, your own son calls you: stand at my side!

ELECTRA: I echo him, with tears that are never dried!

CHORUS: We with one voice repeat the cry he cried:
Hear us, rise to the light
And stand with us against our enemies!

ORESTES: If it be swords,
The God of Swords will strike for us.
If it be judgement,
The God of Judgement will plead for us.

ELECTRA: Hear us, you gods; judge our cause righteously.

CHORUS: I hear your prayers, and tremble.
The appointed end has waited long;
But prayer will accomplish it.

ORESTES: O the curse of our house! Spirit of murder!
Discordant strokes, and blood unnatural!

ELECTRA: Hideous pain, sorrow intolerable!

ALL: Oh, when shall suffering end?

ORESTES: There is no way but this to staunch the wound
That bleeds our race.
None from outside can help; we must ourselves
Cure our own case –

ELECTRA: Since blood must match with blood, and wrong
with wrong.

ALL: We have done. May the powers below accept our song.

CHORUS: Gods of the earthy shade,
Grant all we pray for; aid

The weak against the strong;
Smile on our hopes, and bless
Our deed with full success.

ORESTES: My king, my father, dead by a death no king should
die,

Give me, I pray, this throne and kingdom, yours by right.

ELECTRA: Look on my state, my need. Save me from this re-
proach,

'Sold to Aegisthus'!

ORESTES:                   Save us, and the due ritual feasts
Shall be established for you; else, when the fat of rams
Burns on all altars, you shall alone be portionless.

ELECTRA: And I from my rich dowry, on my wedding-day,
Will pour libations for you from our ancestral store;
And reverence this tomb above all other things.

ORESTES: O Earth, send me my father to direct my sword.

ELECTRA: O send us glorious victory, Queen Persephone.

ORESTES: Remember, father, the holy bath stained with your
blood.

ELECTRA: Remember the cloak – the net they wove to bind
your limbs.

ORESTES: A trap, not of iron, but thread, made you their
prey, my father.

ELECTRA: Robed to your shame in a robe of shameful
treachery.

ORESTES: Are you not roused, my father, with the story of
your reproach?

ELECTRA: Dearest father, will you not rise to deliver us?

ORESTES: Do you not long to defeat those who defeated you?
Then either send forth Justice to enforce our loyal cause,
Or let us grapple in turn, with a grip as fierce as theirs.

ELECTRA: Yet hear this last cry, father; look on us as we sit
Here at your tomb; have pity on your own flesh and blood,
Male and female, through whom alone your race will live.

ORESTES: We are the seed of Pelops; let us not be blotted out.
You are dead – and yet not dead: still you can live in us.

ELECTRA: Children preserve alive a dead man's name and fame.

They are like corks that hold the fisherman's net, and keep
His knotted lines from sinking to the ocean bed.

ORESTES: Our pleas are for your sake. Hear, then, and save yourself.

CHORUS: Come! You have spoken liberally to discharge all duty,

Honouring the grave a hard fate left unwept. But now,
Seeing your will is bent on action, lose no time;
Swiftly to work, and prove the favour of Heaven.

ORESTES: I will.

And yet, it is not idle or dilatory to ask
What made her send forth these libations? Why so late
Must she show scruple for a wrong no care can cure?
Or had the dead no wit, to be sent this paltry sop?
Impossible! Yet – so small an offering for such a crime?
Why, if a man poured out his wealth to the last drop
To atone a single murder, it is labour wasted, they say.
If you can, tell me why she did it. I want to know.

CHORUS: I can tell, son; I was there. It was dreams, night-walking terrors,

That frightened the godless woman and made her send these gifts.

ORESTES: Did you ask what the dream was? Can you describe it clearly?

CHORUS: She told us herself. She dreamt that she gave birth to a snake.

ORESTES: What followed? Or was that all? Tell me the point of it.

CHORUS: She wrapped it in shawls and lulled it to rest like a little child.

ORESTES: Surely this new-born monster needed food – what
food?

CHORUS: She herself, in her dream, gave it her breast to suck.

ORESTES: Her nipple surely was wounded by its loathsome
fang?

CHORUS: Yes; with her milk the creature drew forth clots of
blood.

ORESTES: This dream was sent. It came from her husband,
Agamemnon.

CHORUS: She screamed out in her sleep, and woke in a fit of
trembling;
And through the palace many lamps, that the dark had
dimmed,
Flared up to reassure her. Immediately she sends
Libations, hoping to purge this poison at its source.

ORESTES: I pray, then, to this earth that holds my father's
bones,
That the dream's meaning may be thus fulfilled in me.
As I interpret, point by point it fits. Listen:
First, if this snake came forth from the same place as I,
And, as though human, was then wrapped in infant-clothes,
Its gaping mouth clutching the breast that once fed me;
If it then mingled the sweet milk with curds of blood,
And made her shriek with terror – why, it means that she
Who nursed this obscene beast must die by violence;
*I* must transmute my nature, be viperous in heart and act!
The dream commands it: I am her destined murderer.

CHORUS: I choose your reading of these signs, and say Amen.
We are your friends; now give your orders to each of us;
Tell us what we must do or not do.

ORESTES:                          That is simple.
Electra, you must enter the palace, and disarm
Any suspicion of my plan. It was treachery
They used to kill *him* – they shall find his price was high,

123

When treachery traps and kills *them* in the self-same snare,
According to the prophetic word of Loxias,
Of Lord Apollo, whose oracles never yet have failed.
Now for my plan. Disguised as a foreigner, head to foot,
I shall come with Pylades here to the outer gate of the
    palace,
A 'guest of the house' – a 'guest in arms'. We will cloak our
    tongues
With the Parnassian accent, to seem both men of Phocis.
The doorkeepers, maybe, will greet us with sour looks,
Saying the house is frantic with supernatural fears.
Then we will wait; while passers-by surmise, and say,
'Why does Aegisthus make a suppliant wait outside?
He is at home, and knows.' – But, be that as it may,
Once I set foot inside the palace door, and see
The wretch Aegisthus sitting on my father's throne,
Or if he then comes face to face with me – I tell you,
He is a dead man, let him once but meet my eye.
He'll have no time to ask, 'What man is that?' – but death
From my bronze sword will leap on him and strangle him.
The Fiend murder has glutted in time past, today
Shall drink the third, completing draught of unmixed blood.
Your task, then, sister, is to keep careful watch indoors,
So that our several parts may piece together well.
You women, keep a prudent tongue; speak or be dumb
As each new moment asks. For the rest, I call on Hermes
To follow, witness, guide and bless my sword's ordeal.
        *Exeunt* ORESTES, PYLADES *and* ELECTRA.
CHORUS: Earth teems with fear in countless forms,
        Her nursery a spoilers' den;
        And the deep lap of ocean swarms
        With savage shapes that prey on men;
        Fire glaring from mid-sky at noon
        Strikes feathered wing and furry pelt;

Which both could tell, for both have felt,
The anger of the mad typhoon.

But man's rash heart, his stubborn will,
And woman's desperate love and hate –
Who can set forth their train of ill
Disastrous and insatiate?
For reckless passion, that makes blind
Each female heart, comes thwart and sly
To flout the fond connubial tie
And mock both beasts and human kind.

Learn truth from sad Althaea,
Should your own thought lack wing;
Who steeled her heart to kindle
The fatal torch, well knowing
Whose death the hours would bring
With that flame's guttering.
For by its waning brightness
Her own son's ebbing tide
Was measured, from the moment
He left her womb and cried,
Until the day he died.

As byword for abhorrence
Another name is named:
Scylla, who sent her father
To die where swords were waiting,
And yet was not ashamed.
Bribed with a Cretan collar
That Minos made of gold,
She found him calmly sleeping,
And cut the hair that gave him
The gift the gods withhold;

And Hermes touched his shoulder,
And soon his breath was cold.

Two tales are told of sores no salve can cure;
Hear now the third and worst.
Where marriage harbours hate,
Where woman's brain can plot
Fierce treachery against her warrior mate,
Whose brow his trembling enemies saw
Darkened with majesty and awe –
There stands a house by all the gods accursed!
Honour belongs where home and hearth are pure,
Where neither hate grows hot,
Nor woman's daring impulse reaches
Beyond the bound that virtue teaches.

Yes, of all crimes remembered, one stands first:
The Lemnian massacre, a tale
To make men groan with heartsickness.
And when they speak, all pale,
Of some new outrage, 'It is as bad,' they say,
'As what occurred in Lemnos.' So to this day,
By gods detested, our whole sex is cursed,
By men disfranchised, scorned, and portionless;
For no man honours what the gods abhor.
Three cases prove my point; I'll name no more.

Near the heart the pointed sword
Waits; when Justice gives the word,
Through and through, sour-edged and strong,
Strikes the blade. For none can long
Scorn regard of right and wrong,
Break the holy laws of Heaven,
And hope to find his deed forgiven.

Justice plants her anvil; Fate
Forges keen the brazen knife.
Murder still will propagate
Murder; life must fall for life.
So the avenging Fiend, renowned
For long resolve and guile profound,
Now the wheel has turned with time,
Pays in blood the ancient crime.

*During this Ode the scene has changed to the front of the palace.
Enter* ORESTES *and* PYLADES *with attendants.* ORESTES
*knocks at the palace door.*

ORESTES: Hullo, there! Hear me knocking at your outer
door!

Anyone there, I say? [*He knocks again.*] Is anyone in the
palace?

[*He knocks again.*] Hullo, there, for the third time! Open the
door, will you,

If Aegisthus' house is used to treating strangers well!

*A* SERVANT *appears.*

SERVANT: All right, I can hear you. What's your city? Where
are you from?

ORESTES: Take word to the masters of the house, that I want
to see them,

And deliver them some news. And be quick, for Night
drives on

In her murky car, and it's time for travellers to drop
anchor

At a friendly inn. Ask someone in authority to come –

A woman, if she is in charge; though a man would be more
suitable;

Then there's no talking at cross-purposes out of politeness;

A man's at ease with a man and can show his evidence
plainly.

CLYTEMNESTRA *has appeared at the door.*

CLYTEMNESTRA: Sirs, say what you have to say. This house can offer

All that you would expect – warm baths, and other comforts,

A restful bed, with friendly welcome and entertainment.

If besides this you wish to broach more serious business,

That is matter for men, and I will tell them of it.

ORESTES: I am from Phocis, a Daulian travelling with my own merchandise

To Argos; and here I have just – as it were – unharnessed my legs.

I met a man on the way – a stranger, as I to him –

Whose name, our conversation showed, was Strophius, a Phocian;

He asked me where I was going, and told me about himself;

Then, 'Since you're bound for Argos in any case,' says he,

'Keep in mind this message and deliver it faithfully.

Tell his parents – and don't forget – Orestes is dead.

So, if his family think it best to convey him home,

Or to let him remain our guest, and be buried here in Phocis –

A resident alien, you might say – come back to me

And state their wish. Meanwhile due mourning has been observed,

And now his ashes lie in a stout casket of bronze.'

That was my message. Whether by chance I speak to one

Who, being concerned, can give me my answer, I don't know;

But it's right his parents should be told.

CLYTEMNESTRA:                              Oh, misery!

Our last defences shattered and our life despoiled!

O irresistible curse haunting an unhappy house:

Nothing escapes your watch. We hide away our treasures,

But still you aim from far, and with your keen-eyed arrows

Strip my miserable life of all who are dear to me.
Orestes now – who thought, no doubt, it was wise to keep
His foot out of the deadly swamp – our only hope
To charm the curse of the house from running triumphantly
    amuck –
Now the enrolling Fury records Orestes' name.

ORESTES: I only wish that I could have introduced myself
As a bringer of good news to so royal and rich a house,
And enjoyed its entertainment. The warmest of all friend-
    ship
Is a guest's towards his host; and I would have thought it
    wrong
Not to perform a task like this; for I gave my word,
And now I have been welcomed with much courtesy.

CLYTEMNESTRA: You shall enjoy no less the welcome you
    have earned,
And as our guest call this your home. If you had not come,
Some other man would soon have brought us the same news.
But men who travel all day, and still have far to go,
Must take their time for food and rest. [*To a servant*] Show
    him indoors;
His friend too, and attendants; lodge them comfortably
In the men's quarters, and give them worthy entertainment.
Be exact and diligent; you will be held responsible.
– I will report this news to the king; and with our friends –
For we have many – we will discuss the situation.

                    *All go into the palace.*

CHORUS: Come, women! Soon our hearts must nerve
        Our tongues to speak, and show that we
        Though weak, are loyal, and can serve
        Orestes in emergency.

        O earth revered, O sacred mound
        That grief and love for mourning made,

Sad covering for the King of Fleets,
Now hear our prayer, now send your aid.
Now let Persuasion use her cheats
And join the fight! Let Hermes, lord
Of secret powers below the ground,
Safeguard and whet the perilous sword!


It seems our Daulian guest is causing trouble. Look!
Here comes Orestes' nurse, dissolved in tears. Cilissa!
What are you doing, coming out by the palace gate,
And hand in hand with sorrow? These tears are not hired.

*An old woman has come out of the palace.*

NURSE: My lady told me to fetch Aegisthus straight away,
   To hear from the men themselves this news we've just been
      told,
   This terrible news. There's a sad look in her false eyes,
   Put on before us servants; underneath she laughs –
   Why not? – for her, this business has been managed well;
   Though, for our house – these men's report seems plain
      enough –
   It spells disaster. How he'll hug himself for joy,
   That creature, when he hears of it! Oh, oh, my grief!
   How cruel and bitter that first dose of trouble seemed,
   When Atreus ruled this palace; how my heart bled then!
   And yet I never felt a blow so hard as this.
   I've met with trouble, borne it to the bitter end;
   But my Orestes! . . . Bless his heart, he wore me out.
   I reared him, took him new-born from his mother's arms.
   And oh! the times he shouted at me in the night,
   Made me get up, and bothered me with this and that –
   And all my hopes for nothing! Why, you understand,
   A baby knows no better; you must nurse it, then,
   Like a dumb animal, whatever way seems best.
   A child in the cradle can't explain what troubles it;

Whether it wants to eat, to drink, or to make water,
A baby's inside takes no orders; it's too young.
Well, often I could tell; and often, too, I know,
I guessed it wrong; and then I'd have to wash his things,
For nurse and laundress both were the same pair of hands.
So I did double duty; yes, and I brought up
Orestes for his father. And now, to hear of this,
Orestes dead! Now I must go to fetch the man,
The curse and shame of the house; and pleased he'll be to hear.

CHORUS: How does your message say he is to come? In state?

NURSE: In state? Say that again, please; I don't understand.

CHORUS: Is he to come with an armed escort, or alone?

NURSE: Oh; yes, with an armed escort.

CHORUS:                                         Nurse: say no such thing
To our detested master. Go as quick as you can,
Put on a cheerful air and tell him to come alone
So that the men may tell their story without fear.
*A wise messenger makes a crooked message straight.*

NURSE: What's this? Do you, then, welcome what we've heard today?

CHORUS: What if at long last Zeus should make the ill wind change?

NURSE: Change? How? Orestes was our hope; and now he's gone.

CHORUS: It takes a clever prophet to be sure of that.

NURSE: What do you mean? Have you heard something different, then?

CHORUS: Go, take your message; do what you were told to do.
The gods will see to matters that concern the gods.

*Exit* NURSE.

CHORUS: Zeus, Father of Olympian gods, I pray,
Grant now – now! – that the fortunes of this house

Be planted firm; that those whose righteous vows
Plead for sound rule, may see their hopes today.
This prayer we make
For holy Justice' sake;
Keep Justice still our shield and stay.

> The prince is in the hall.
> Zeus, set him face to face with the enemy!
> If you exalt him to greatness,
> You shall receive, if you will,
> Twofold and threefold sacrifice of thanksgiving.

The orphan son of one whom you held dear,
O Zeus, is harnessed for a deadly race;
Then for his running measure such a space
As one may run on ground level and clear,
In rhythmic stride,
And so on swift steps ride
Triumphant to the winning-place.

Gods of the inmost hearth, where smiling wealth
Draws blessing from your power, with favour hear!
Cancel the doom for crimes long past which hold
This house imprisoned in perpetual fear.
Re-try our case; this guilty blood is old,
And should be sterile, and the house find health.

> Lord of the lovely temple in the deep cave,
> Apollo, grant that this house
> May raise its eyes from the dust,
> And welcome a man for its master.
> Let the gloomy veil be parted,
> Let noble deeds be crowned in glory,
> And the house shine forth with blessing!

And Hermes, son of Maia, will surely be
Our ally – none so fair a following wind
To speed our action, if his will be kind.
Often he wins advantage stealthily;
Subtle, elusive is his speech, to pull
Night's curtain on his ways and make men blind;
Yet no more palpable when day shines full.

Then, then the hour will come
When we shall change our shrill lament
To that triumphal air
Chanted by women when the wind sets fair,
Hymning the liberation of our royal home:
'A new day rises for our city's life;
My own heart warms for blessing sent;
And friends are freed from haunting fear and strife!'

    Keep a bold heart, Orestes!
    When the moment comes to kill her,
    Thunder your father's killing;
    When she whimpers, 'Child, Orestes!'
    Answer, 'I am – my father's!'
    Finish your fearful deed;
    It is fate, and none condemns you.

Plant in your steadfast breast
The hardened heart that Perseus bore.
For sake of those you love,
Below earth and above,
Exact amends to soothe their wrath to rest.
Now for the house of Atreus win
By your dread, final deed
Redemption from within;
That ancient feuds may bleed no more,
Now utterly destroy their source and seed!

*Enter* AEGISTHUS.

AEGISTHUS: Well, I have come, seeing a message was sent to
    call me.

    Disturbing news – and most unwelcome – is, I hear,

    Alleged by certain travellers, of Orestes' death.

    But to impute this too to our house's evil destiny

    Would be to burden a back now galled and festering

    From murders past, with a new weight of sweating fear.

    Well, what am I to think? Is this the living truth?

    Or gossip born of female panic, flaring high,

    And soon dying to nothing? Give me a reasoned answer.

CHORUS: Indeed we heard this news. But ask the men them-
    selves –

    They are in the house. No news is sure at second-hand;

    Better to find the truth by asking man to man.

AEGISTHUS: I'll see this traveller, and learn by further ques-
    tioning

    Whether he was there in person when Orestes died,

    Or picked up some dim rumour and purveys it here.

    He'll not get past a man with two eyes and five wits.

          AEGISTHUS *goes into the palace.*

CHORUS: Great Zeus, what can I say?

    I must pray – but where begin?

    Spirit and will are urgent

    For a prayer to match the moment,

    A cry to appeal and win!

    The human victim's ready,

    The knife is near to the skin –

    But what will end the day?

    Either annihilation

    Utter and everlasting

    For the house of Agamemnon;

    Or with the flame of freedom,

    The light of our salvation,

Our prince will purge his throne,
And rule the land with justice
And in wealth enjoy his own.
Such is the fearful issue
This moment must decide;
One against two, Orestes
Takes up the grim succession,
And God is on his side;
May right by victory be justified!

*A shriek of death is heard from inside the palace;*
*it is the voice of* AEGISTHUS.

CHORUS: Whose voice was it? Who has won? Who rules the
palace now?

Come, stand aside, till we know more. We must not appear
As accomplices. The fight is over, the die cast.

*The scene changes to the inner court. On one side is a door leading to*
*the guests' quarters; in the centre, that leading to the women's*
*quarters. From the former a* SERVANT *of Aegisthus rushes in.*

SERVANT: Help, help! My master's dead! He's dead!
Aegisthus, dead!

Open at once! Unbar the women's doors, I say!
Come quickly, someone strong! Not that there's any hope
Of helping; it's all over. Open there! Hullo!
Help! Can't you hear me? Are you all deaf, or fast asleep?
Where's Clytemnestra? What's she doing? Like as not
She'll get her own throat cut – she's on the razor's edge!

*Enter* CLYTEMNESTRA.

CLYTEMNESTRA: What is all this? Why are you making this
disturbance?

SERVANT: The dead, I tell you, come to life to kill the
living!

CLYTEMNESTRA: The dead? O gods, the dead! Yes, I know
who you mean.

It is true, we killed by craft; by craft we are now to die.

Run, bring me a weapon. [*Exit* SERVANT.] Let us know
now, win or lose!

The whole long, bitter story reaches its final turn.

*Enter* ORESTES.

ORESTES: Yes, it is you I seek. His score, in there, is paid.

CLYTEMNESTRA: What? Oh, dearest Aegisthus! Dead?
Where was your strength?

ORESTES: Was he dear, this man of yours? Good: you shall
lie with him

In the grave; then, though he's dead, you will never be
false to him.

CLYTEMNESTRA: Down with your sword, my son!

     ORESTES *does not move;* CLYTEMNESTRA *kneels.*

               My own child, see this breast:
Here often your head lay, in sleep, while your soft mouth
Sucked from me the good milk that gave you life and
strength.

*Enter* PYLADES.

ORESTES: Pylades, what shall I do? To kill a mother is terrible.
Shall I show mercy?

PYLADES:         Where then are Apollo's words,
His Pythian oracles? What becomes of men's sworn oaths?
Make all men living your enemies, but not the gods.

ORESTES: I uphold your judgement; your advice is good. [*To*
CLYTEMNESTRA] Come on;

I mean to kill you close beside him. While he lived
You preferred him to my father. Sleep with him in death;
For you love him, and hate the man you should have loved.

CLYTEMNESTRA: I gave you your life: let me then live out
my own.

ORESTES: Live? Here, in my house – you, my father's mur-
derer?

CLYTEMNESTRA: My child, Fate played a part; I was not all
to blame.

ORESTES: Then here's another death decreed by the same Fate.

CLYTEMNESTRA: My son, do you not fear a parent's curse?

ORESTES:                                        A parent!
You bore me; then discarded me to misery.

CLYTEMNESTRA: Sent you to trusted friends. Was that discarding you?

ORESTES: I was born free: you sold my body and my throne.

CLYTEMNESTRA: Sold? Where is any price I got for selling you?

ORESTES: Your price? I will not name him, for I blush for you.

CLYTEMNESTRA: Your father sinned too. Count his sins along with mine.

ORESTES: Silence! He spent himself in battle, you sat at home.

CLYTEMNESTRA: A woman without her man suffers no less, my son.

ORESTES: The man's work keeps and feeds the woman who sits at home.

CLYTEMNESTRA: Are you resolved, my son, to murder your own mother?

ORESTES: It will be your own hand that strikes you dead, not mine.

CLYTEMNESTRA: Beware the hounding Furies of a mother's curse.

ORESTES: How shall I escape my father's curse if I relent?

CLYTEMNESTRA: *The living wail to the dead:* it is true, I waste my breath.

ORESTES: The wind of Fate blows straight from my father's death to yours.

CLYTEMNESTRA: My dream – O gods! Here is the snake I bore and fed.

ORESTES: The terror in your dream told you prophetic truth.
Unholy was your crime, unholy shall be your punishment.

ORESTES *drives* CLYTEMNESTRA *into the palace;*
PYLADES *follows.*

CHORUS: I mourn even for these two, one in their guilt, their
    end.
  Yet, since our prince has crowned the murderous past with
    blood
  To his own pain, I welcome, of two choices, this:
  That the dear hope of Argos is not sunk in death.

    As to the sons of Priam slow but sure
    Judgement with heavy retribution came,
    So to this palace double death pursued
    The twofold beast that reigned and ravaged there.
    The exile prayed; the god instructed well;
    The avenger sped unflinching to his goal.

      Sing joy! Cry victory!
      This glorious day has set
      The throne of Argos free,
      Made smooth her rough road, and will yet
      Restore the wealth stripped bare
      By that guilt-ridden pair.

  The hand that wields a hidden sword at last
  Falls overreached by hidden punishment.
  She whom men rightly call Zeus' daughter, Justice,
  Even as he struck, guided Orestes' arm,
  And breath of her wrath quelled his enemies.

      Sing joy! Cry victory!
      This glorious day has set
      The throne of Argos free,
      Made smooth her rough road, and will yet
      Restore the wealth stripped bare
      By that guilt-ridden pair.

Apollo, lord of the great temple-cave
Below Parnassus, thundered forth his word:
*Use falsehood – but my word shall not prove false.*
Justice in her good time
Now ratifies the word Apollo gave.
For thus, it seems, the powers of Heaven prevail,
Leaving man God-forsaken in his crime.
We then do well to reverence
The rule of God's omnipotence.

Lift your eyes to the day,
Souls of this house! Be strong!
Your chains are thrown away:
Rise up, stand free, and fill
The air with joy. Too long
You lay prostrate and still.

Soon time accomplished and accomplishing
Will make glad entry through this royal door,
When once the hearth is purged, the curse untied,
And life is clean once more.
Soon the cast dice will show their lucky side;
Many shall see, and many asked shall tell
The blessings of this house, where Fortune loves to dwell.

*The scene changes to reveal* ORESTES *standing by the dead bodies of*
AEGISTHUS *and* CLYTEMNESTRA. *Attendants are holding
the blood-stained robe in which* CLYTEMNESTRA *entangled*
AGAMEMNON.

ORESTES: Come all and see this sight! These two oppressed
the land,
Murdered my father, plundered my inheritance.
In life they shared one dignity, one throne, one love;
Now, with that dignity, that love, they share one death.

They swore one oath to kill my father miserably;
Likewise, to die together. Both these oaths they kept.

        ORESTES *points to the blood-stained robe.*

  See too this evidence, you judges of my case:
This neat device, the snare in which they trapped my father,
Fettered and pinioned hand and foot. [*To Attendants*] Come,
    spread it out.
See, this was used to truss a man; a strait-jacket.
Stand round and show it. Let the Father see this thing –
Not mine, but him whose eye beholds all deeds on earth:
Let the Sun see this horror that was my mother's work!
Then let him witness for me, when I come to trial,
That right and duty forced my hands to do this murder –
I mean my mother's; *his* death gets no word from me –
He has the law's provision for adulterers.
But she who planned *this* filthy crime [*pointing to the robe*]
    against a husband,
Whose child she carried in her body, and once loved,
Though now you see him as her cruel enemy –
What of her? If she had been a sting-ray or an adder,
Her sole touch, without fangs, would have gangrened some
    victim
In virtue of mere savagery and natural venom.
What shall I call this, even if I search for euphemism?
A trap for a wild beast? Or a corpse's winding-strip
Covering his coffined feet? A net, perhaps; a gin;
A hobbled gown for crippling. Some ingenious bandit,
Professional cutpurse, might make such an instrument
To outwit poor travellers, and with this nice villainy
Murder away, and smoulder at the heart with guilt. . . .
With such a woman may I never share my home;
Sooner than that, may the gods send me childless death!
CHORUS: I weep for the king you killed;
    I weep for your end fulfilled.

Your death was a fearful thing;
Yet when time has waited long
There grows from the root of wrong
The flower of suffering.

ORESTES: Is she guilty or not guilty? See this robe dyed red
From the work of Aegisthus' sword: there is my evidence.
Yes, it is blood – blood, whose stains have joined with time
To fade and corrode the colours of this patterned stuff.

Now I pronounce the praise I could not utter then;
I offer now my lament, since I may not see his body,
To this treacherous web that caught and killed my father.

Her deed, her punishment – the whole business tortures
    me!
A victory whose pollution makes my life abhorred.

CHORUS: No man may hope to spend
His life untouched by pain
And favoured to the end.
Some griefs are with us now; others again
Time and the gods will send.

ORESTES: Now listen. At this moment I am like a man
Driving a team of horses and not knowing where
The gallop's going to end. My wits chafe at the rein
Under my weakened grip, and carry me off the course;
Terror begins to sing at my heart and set it dancing
In anger. Therefore, while I am still in my right mind,
To all who are loyal to me I solemnly proclaim:
It was no sin to kill my mother, who was herself
Marked with my father's blood, unclean, abhorred by gods.
And, for the spells that nerved me to this dreadful act,
I offer, in full warrant, Apollo Loxias,
Who from his Pythian oracle revealed to me
That if I did this deed I should be clear of blame;

If I neglected it – I will not tell the penance;
Such torments lie far beyond bowshot of man's mind.


   See what I do now. Fore-armed with this branch, this
      wreath,
I will go as suppliant to Apollo's holy ground,
Where in the temple of earth's centre the lamp gleams
With the immortal flame; and there seek refuge, exiled
For the shedding of this kindred blood. That way, no other,
Apollo bade me turn for help. As for this act,
I call upon all Argive men in time to come
To bear me witness, that the death she suffered here
Was not by me inflicted in mere ruthlessness.
Let this be the report held of me as I go
Forth from my native land an exiled wanderer.

CHORUS: Right and success are with you; then why clog your
   tongue
   With inauspicious words? You have set Argos free,
   And all her people; the two beasts that plagued us fell
   Helpless before your sword. Why speak of ill to come?

ORESTES [seeing the Furies approach]: Ah, ah!
   Look, women, see them, there! Like Gorgons, with grey
      cloaks,
   And snakes coiled swarming round their bodies! Let me go!

CHORUS: Most loyal of sons, what fancied sights torment you
   so?
   Stay! You have won your victory; what have you to fear?

ORESTES: To me these living horrors are not imaginary;
   I know them – avenging hounds incensed by a mother's
     blood.

CHORUS: That blood is still a fresh pollution on your hands,
   Therefore your mind's distracted. What more natural?

ORESTES: O Lord Apollo! More and more of them! Look
   there!

And see – their dreadful eyes dripping with bloody pus!

CHORUS: Go quickly then where cleansing waits for you;
    stretch out

Your hand to Apollo, and he will free you from this torment.

ORESTES: I know you do not see these beings; but I see them.
    I am lashed and driven! I can't bear it! I must escape!

*    With a cry of agony* ORESTES *rushes away.*

CHORUS: Good fortune go with you; and may the blessing of
    God

Watch over and guide your ways, and bring you peace in the
    end.

*    The* CHORUS *group themselves at the front of
    the stage to address the audience.*

The ancient curse thus for the third time brings
A hurricane's havoc on this house of kings;
    Now, its destruction done,
    The tempest's course is run.


Thyestes' murdered children first began
This doom. Next in succession died a man,
Lord of Achaean armies, brave and good,
    Whom treachery cut down as he stood
    Naked to cleanse his soul of blood.


    Now unforeseen the third
    Comes – and we hold our breath
    Seeking the hopeful word –
Act of deliverance? Or one more death?


When shall be solved this long feud's argument?
    When shall the ancestral curse relent,
    And sink to rest, its fury spent?

# THE EUMENIDES

*

CHARACTERS:

THE PYTHIAN PRIESTESS
APOLLO
HERMES
ORESTES
THE GHOST OF CLYTEMNESTRA
CHORUS *of the Furies, or Eumenides*
ATHENE
*Twelve Athenian Citizens*
*A number of Athenian women and girls*

*

*Scene: First at Delphi, at the Pythian Oracle, or Temple of Apollo;
then at Athens, in the Temple of Athene on the Acropolis.*
*Scene 1: Before the Pythian Oracle. The scene is curtained.* THE
PYTHIAN PRIESTESS *enters below at one side, mounts by steps
to the stage, and stands at the centre before the curtain.*
PRIESTESS: First in my prayer of all the gods I reverence
Earth, first author of prophecy; Earth's daughter then,
Themis; who, legend tells, next ruled this oracle;
The third enthroned, succeeding by good-will, not force,
Phoebe – herself another Titan child of Earth –
In turn gave her prerogative, a birthday gift,
To her young namesake, Phoebus. From the Delian lake
Ringed with high rocks he came to the craft-crowded
   shores
Of Pallas; thence to Parnassus and this holy seat.
And in his progress bands of Attic worshippers,
Hephaestus' sons, builders of roads, escorted him,

Taming for pilgrims' passage ground untamed before.
So Phoebus came to Delphi; people and king alike
Paid him high honour; Zeus endowed his prescient mind
With heavenly wisdom, and established him as fourth
Successor to this throne, whence he, as Loxias,
Interprets to mankind his father's word and will.

These first my piety invokes. And I salute
With holy words Pallas Pronaia, and the nymphs
Of the Corycian cave, where, in enchanted shelter,
Birds love to nest; where Bromius too makes his home,
Since, once, he led his frenzied Bacchic army forth
To tear King Pentheus as a hare is torn by hounds.
Fountains of Pleistos, Delphi's river, next I name;
Poseidon; and, last, the supreme Fulfiller, Zeus.

Now on the seat of prophecy I take my place;
Heaven grant that this day's service far surpass in blessing
All former days! Let any Greek enquirer here,
As custom is, cast lots for precedence, and come.
As Phoebus guides my lips, so I pronounce his truth.
*The* PRIESTESS *goes in between the curtains. After a short pause,
her voice is heard in a cry of terror, and she reappears.*
A fearful sight, a thing appalling to describe,
Drives me staggering and helpless out of Apollo's house.
My legs give way and tremble; hands must hold me up.
How useless fear makes an old woman – like a child!
As I went towards the inner shrine, all hung with wreaths,
There on the navel-stone a suppliant was sitting,
A man polluted – blood still wet on hands that grasp
A reeking sword; yet on his head fresh olive-leaves,
Twined thickly with white wool, show heedful reverence.
So far I can speak plainly. But beside this man,
Stretched upon benches, sleeping, a strange company

Of women – no, not women; Gorgons – yet, again,
They are not like Gorgons. Harpies I saw painted once,
Monsters robbing King Phineus of his feast; but these
Are wingless, black, utterly loathsome; their vile breath
Vents in repulsive snoring; from their eyes distils
A filthy rheum; their garb is wickedness to wear
In sight of the gods' statues or in human homes.
They are creatures of no race I ever saw; no land
Could breed them and not bear the curse of God and man.
I will go. Loxias is powerful, and this temple's his.
Men's tainted walls wait for his purifying power:
Let him – Priest, Prophet, Healer – now protect his own.

*The* PRIESTESS *returns by the way that she came. The curtains open,*
*revealing the Temple of Apollo. In the centre* ORESTES *sits by a*
*rough stone altar – the 'Navel-Stone'. Beside him stand* APOLLO
*and* HERMES. *Around them, asleep on benches or on the floor,*
*lie the twelve* FURIES.

APOLLO: I will not fail you. Near at hand or far away,
I am your constant guardian and your enemies' dread.
Now for this one brief hour you see these ragers quiet,
These hunters caught in sleep; these ancient, ageless hags,
Whose presence neither god nor man nor beast can bear.
For sake of evil they were born; and evil is
The dark they dwell in, subterranean Tartarus;
Beings abhorred by men and by Olympian gods.
Then fly, and do not weaken. They will hound you yet
Through seas and island cities, over the vast continent,
Wherever the earth's face is hard with wanderers' feet.
Keep courage firm; nurse your appointed pain; and go
To Athens, city of Pallas. There with suppliant hands
Embrace her ancient image, and implore her help.
There I will set you judges; and with soothing pleas
I, who first bade you take your mother's life, will bring
From all your painful days final deliverance.

ORESTES: Apollo, Lord! Knowledge of justice and of right
　　Is yours: let will prompt knowledge, and let care fulfil.
　　Your strength shall be my surety for your promised help.
APOLLO: Remember, let no fear conquer your steadfast heart.
　　Go, Hermes, brother, as his guardian, and fulfil
　　Your titular office. His protection is my care:
　　Shepherd him well. The outlaw has his sanctity,
　　Which Zeus regards, giving him Fortune for his guide.
HERMES *leads* ORESTES *away;* APOLLO *retires into the temple.*
　　THE GHOST OF CLYTEMNESTRA *appears.*
CLYTEMNESTRA: Will you still sleep? Oh, wake! What use
　　are you, asleep?
　　Since you so slight me, I am abused unceasingly
　　Among the other dead, for him I killed, and wander
　　Despised and shamed. I tell you truly, by them all
　　I am held guilty and condemned; while, for the blow
　　My own son struck, no angry voice protests. See here,
　　This wound under my heart, and say whose was the sword!
　　Look! For though daylight cannot see beyond the flesh,
　　The mind in sleep has eyes. Often for you my hand
　　Has poured wineless libations, sober soothing draughts;
　　Upon my hearth in midnight ritual – an hour
　　Given to no other god – banquets have burned for you.
　　Now all my gifts I see spurned underfoot; while he,
　　Like a fawn lightly leaping out of the sprung snare,
　　Has escaped away and gone, and mocks you to your shame.
　　Listen, you Powers of the deep earth, and understand!
　　Listen, I entreat you, for my plea is life and death!
　　Listen! In your dream I, Clytemnestra, call to you!
　　　*The* CHORUS *mutter restlessly, as dogs growl in sleep.*
CLYTEMNESTRA: You murmur; but your prey has vanished
　　out of sight.
　　His friends are not like mine: they save him, while you
　　sleep.

*Again the* CHORUS *mutter.*

CLYTEMNESTRA: Will you not wake? Does grief not touch
  you? He has gone!

Orestes, who killed me, his mother, has escaped!

*More excited cries come from the* CHORUS.

CLYTEMNESTRA: Still crying, still asleep? Quick now, wake
  and stand up!

To work! Evil's your province – evil waits for you!

*The cries continue.*

CLYTEMNESTRA: Sleep and fatigue, two apt accomplices,
  have drained

All force from the she-dragons' rage.

CHORUS [*with still louder cries*]: After him! Catch him, catch
  him, catch him, catch him, catch him! Take care, take care!

CLYTEMNESTRA: In dreams you hunt your prey, baying like
  hounds whose thought

Will never rest; but what of deeds? Has weariness

Conquered and softened you with sleep, till you forget

My pain? Rise up, torment his heart with just reproach;

For whetted words goad the quick conscience. Storm at him

With hot blood-reeking blasts blown from your vaporous
  womb,

Wither his hope of respite, hunt him to the death!

*As the* CHORUS *awake, the* GHOST OF CLYTEMNESTRA
  *vanishes.*

CHORUS: Come, wake; wake you too; wake each other;
  come, wake all!

Shake off your sleep, stand up. What could that warning
  mean?

*They see that* ORESTES *has gone.*

What has happened? Furies, we are foiled!

  Who were ever mocked as we?

  Who would bear such mockery?

  Sleepless labour spent in vain!

Duty flouted, privilege despoiled!
    See the empty snare – our prey
    Vanished, fled, and free again!
While we slept our right was stolen away.


Phoebus, son of Zeus, are you a god?
    You set honesty aside;
    You, the younger, ride roughshod
Over elder Powers; you have defied
    Justice for your altar's sake,
    Saved a godless matricide
    From appointed pain, to make
    Mockery of motherhood:
Who can call such crooked dealing good?


Out of my dreams I heard
    A sharp accusing word
That struck me to the deep heart's core,
    As on an uphill road
    The driver's firm-gripped goad
    Strikes till the flesh is sore.
I feel the common scourge, Remorse,
    Wielded in Fate's strong hand,
    Whose cold and crushing force
        None can withstand.


The fault's not ours. It lies
    With younger gods who rise
In place of those that ruled before;
    From stool to crown their throne
        Is stained with gore.
See, how Earth's central sacred stone
    Has taken for its own
A grim pollution Justice must abhor!

Phoebus, for all your prophet's skill,
Your holy wisdom, by this deed
You of your own unprompted will
Have sullied your own altar's flames,
Infringing laws by gods decreed
And Destiny's primeval claims,
To grant some mortal's passing need.

Fate's enemy, my enemy too,
Shall not give sanctuary to sin.
Orestes is accurst, and he,
Though he seek refuge with the dead,
Shall find no place where guilt is free;
Soon there shall come, of his own kin,
A like Avenger, to renew
Fate's curse upon his branded head.

*Enter* APOLLO *from within the temple, carrying his bow and quiver.*

APOLLO: Out of this temple! I command you, go at once!
Quit my prophetic sanctuary, lest you feel
The gleaming snake that darts winged from my golden bow,
And painfully spew forth the black foam that you suck
From the sour flesh of murderers. What place have you
Within these walls? Some pit of punishments, where heads
Are severed, eyes torn out, throats cut, manhood unmanned,
Some hell of maimings, mutilations, stonings, where
Bodies impaled on stakes melt the mute air with groans –
Your place is there! Such are the feasts you love, for which
Heaven loathes you. Is not this the truth, proclaimed in you
By every feature? Find some blood-gorged lion's den,
There make your seemly dwelling, and no more rub off
Your foulness in this house of prayer and prophecy.
Away! Graze other fields, you flock unshepherded!
No god loves such as you!

CHORUS:                    Now is my turn to speak.

You, Lord Apollo, you alone are answerable
To your own charge; what's done's your doing, first to last.

APOLLO: How's this? So far inform me.

CHORUS:                                It was your oracle
That bade him take his mother's life.

APOLLO:                                My oracle
Bade him avenge his father.

CHORUS:                        With his hand still red
He found you his protector.

APOLLO:                        I commanded him
To fly for refuge to this temple.

CHORUS:                                We are here
As his appointed escort. Why revile us then?

APOLLO: Your presence here is outrage.

CHORUS:                                But it is no less
Our duty and our office.

APOLLO:                A high office, this.
Come, with due pride proclaim it.

CHORUS:                                We hound matricides
To exile.

APOLLO: And when wife kills husband, what of her?

CHORUS: They are not kin; therefore such blood is not self-
    spilt.

APOLLO: Then you dishonour and annul the marriage-bond
Of Zeus and Hera, that confirms all marriage-bonds;
And by your argument the sweetest source of joy
To mortals, Aphrodite, falls into contempt.
Marriage, that joins two persons in Fate's ordinance,
Guarded by justice, stands more sacred than an oath.
If, then, to one that kills the other you show grace,
All penalty remitted, and all wrath renounced,
You are unjust to persecute Orestes' life.
*His* crime, I know, you take most grievously to heart;
While for his mother's you show open leniency.

Pallas herself shall hear this case, and judge our pleas.
CHORUS: I tell you, I will never let Orestes go.
APOLLO: Pursue him, then; take all the pains you wish.
CHORUS:                                              Phoebus,
You shall not, even in word, curtail my privilege.
APOLLO: Not as a gift would I accept your privilege.
CHORUS: You are called great beside the throne of Zeus.
   But I
Will trace him by his mother's blood, hound him to earth,
And sue for justice on him.
APOLLO:                           He is my suppliant;
And I will stand by him and save him if I can.
Fierce anger stirs to action both in heaven and earth
If I forsake the guilty man who turned to me.
   *While* APOLLO *speaks the* CHORUS *have begun to leave the*
      *stage;* APOLLO *withdraws into the temple.*


*Scene II: The Temple of Athene in Athens, with a statue of the goddess*
   *before it.* ORESTES *enters and kneels before the statue.*
ORESTES: Divine Athene! At Apollo's word I come.
Receive me graciously; though still a fugitive,
Not unclean now. Long wandering through tribes and towns
Has cleansed my bloodstained hand, blunted the edge of
   guilt;
Welcoming homes have rubbed the foulness from my soul.
Now, my long journey over land and sea fulfilled,
Faithful to Loxias' bidding and his oracle,
Goddess, I approach your house, your holy effigy.
Here I will stay, to know the issue of my trial.
   *The* CHORUS *enter, following the track of* ORESTES.
CHORUS: This is his trail, I have it clear. Come, follow, where
The silent finger of pollution points the way.
Still by the scent we track him, as hounds track a deer
Wounded and bleeding. As a shepherd step by step

Searches a mountain, so have we searched every land,
Flown wingless over sea, swifter than sailing ships,
Always pursuing, till we gasp with weariness.
Now he is here, I know, crouched in some hiding-place.
The scent of mortal murder laughs in my nostrils –

Look there! See him! See him at last!
Watch every doorway, lest the murderer
Steal away and escape unpunished!
Once again he has found protection;
Closely clinging to the immortal
Goddess's image, thus he offers
His life for trial, for the deed of his hand.

No hope can rescue him.
A mother's blood once spilt
None can restore again;
In dust the fresh stream lies,
A parched, accusing stain.
You shall, for your soul's guilt,
Give us your blood to drink
Red from the living limb,
Our dear and deadly food,
Our labour's lawful prize.
Yes, while you still draw breath,
Your withered flesh shall sink,
In payment for her blood,
In penance for her pain,
Down to the world of death.

Mark this: not only you,
But every mortal soul
Whose pride has once transgressed
The law of reverence due

To parent, god, or guest,
Shall pay sin's just, inexorable toll.

Deep in the nether sky
Death rules the ways of man
With stern and strong control;
And there is none who can,
By any force or art,
Elude Death's watchful eye
Or his recording heart.

ORESTES: Long taught by pain, learned in cleansing ritual,
I know when speech is lawful, when to hold my tongue;
And in this case a wise instructor bade me speak.
The blood upon my hands is drowsed and quenched; the
    stain
Of matricide washed clean, exorcized while yet fresh
At Phoebus' hearth with purgative blood-offerings.
It would take long to tell of all the friends whose homes
And hands have given me welcome without harm or taint.
And now from holy lips, with pure words, I invoke
Athene, ruler of this country, to my aid.
Thus she shall gain, without one blow, by just compact,
Myself, my country, and my Argive citizens
In loyal, lasting, unreserved confederacy.
Whether by the Tritonian lake, her Libyan home,
She stands – at rest, at war, a bulwark to her friends;
Or with a warrior's eye in bold command surveys
The Phlegraean plain – a god can hear me – let her now
Come in divine authority and save my soul!

CHORUS: Neither Apollo nor Athene can have power
To save you. Lost, cast off, the very taste of joy
Forgotten, you will live the prey of vampire Powers,
A pale ghost. Do you spurn my words in silence – you,
To me assigned and dedicated? There's no need

To await knife and altar, for your living flesh
Shall feast us. Hear this song that binds you to our will.

Come, Furies, our resolve is set;
Let mime and measure tread their course,
That none who feels the maddening force
Of our dread music may forget
How all the varying fates that bind
Men's lives are by our will assigned.

We hold our judgement just and true:
The man whose open hands are pure
Anger of ours shall not pursue;
He lives untroubled and secure.
But when a sinner, such as he,
Burdened with blood so foully shed,
Covers his guilty hands for shame,
Then, bearing witness for the dead,
We at his judgement stand to claim
The price of blood unyieldingly.

Hear me, O brooding Night,
My mother, from whose womb
I came for punishment
Of all who live in light
Or grope beyond the tomb.
Phoebus would steal away
My office and my right,
My trapped and cowering prey
Whose anguish must atone
For sin so violent,
For blood that bore his own.

*Now, by the altar,*
*Over the victim*

*Ripe for our ritual,*
*Sing this enchantment:*
*A song without music,*
*A sword in the senses,*
*A storm in the heart*
*And a fire in the brain;*
*A clamour of Furies*
*To paralyse reason,*
*A tune full of terror,*
*A drought in the soul!*

Fate, whose all-powerful sway
Weaves out the world's design,
Decreed for evermore
This portion to be mine:
When for some murderous blow
The pangs of guilt surprise
Man's folly, from that day
Close at his side we go
Until the day he dies;
And Hope, that says, 'Below
The earth is respite', lies.

*Now, by the altar,*
*Over the victim*
*Ripe for our ritual,*
*Sing this enchantment:*
*A song without music,*
*A sword in the senses,*
*A storm in the heart*
*And a fire in the brain:*
*A clamour of Furies*
*To paralyse reason,*
*A tune full of terror,*
*A drought in the soul!*

The day we were begotten
These rights to us were sealed,
That against sin of mortals
Our hand should be revealed.
Immortals need.not fear us;
Our feasts no god can share;
When white robes throng the temples
The darkness that we wear
Forbids our presence there.
Our chosen part is torment,
And great ones' overthrow;
When War turns home, and kinsman
Makes kinsman's life-blood flow,
Then in his strength we hunt him
And lay his glory low.

Our zeal assumes this office,
Our care and pains pursue it,
That gods may be exempt;
Zeus, free from taint or question,
Repels our gory presence
With loathing and contempt.
For him our dreaded footfall,
Launched from the height, leaps downward
With keen and crushing force,
Till helpless guilt, despairing,
Falls in his headlong course.

And so men's glories, towering to the sky,
Soon at our black-robed onset, the advance
Of vengeance beating in our fateful dance,
Fade under earth, and in dishonour die.

And in man's downfall his own hand's pollution,
Hovering round him like a misty gloom,

Pours deeper darkness on his mind's confusion,
While groaning ghosts intone his house's doom.

For Law lives on; and we, Law's holy few,
Law's living record of all evil done,
Resourceful and accomplishing, pursue
Our hateful task unhonoured; and no prayer
Makes us relent. All other gods must shun
The sunless glimmer of those paths we strew
With rocks, that quick and dead may stumble there.

So, Heaven's firm ordinance has now been told,
The task which Fate immutably assigned
To our devotion. Who will then withhold
Due fear and reverence? Though our dwelling lie
In subterranean caverns of the blind,
Our ancient privilege none dares deny.

*Enter* ATHENE *from her temple.*

ATHENE: From far away I heard my name loudly invoked,
Beside Scamander, where I went in haste to claim
Land that the Achaean chieftains had allotted me,
An ample gift chosen from plunder won in war
And given entire to Theseus' sons to hold for ever.
And quickly, without toil of foot or wing, I came
Borne on my strident aegis, with the galloping winds
Harnessed before me.

This strange company I see
Here in my precincts moves me – not indeed to fear,
But to amazement. Who are you? I speak to all –
This man who clasps my statue as a suppliant,
And you – beings like none I know that earth brings forth,
Either of those seen among gods and goddesses –
Nor yet are you like mortals. – But I am unjust;
Reason forbids to slander others unprovoked.

CHORUS: Daughter of Zeus, you shall hear all, and briefly
   told.
   We are the children of primeval Night; we bear
   The name of Curses in our home deep under earth.

ATHENE: Your race I know, also your names in common
   speech.

CHORUS: Maybe. Next you shall hear our office.

ATHENE:                                        Willingly;
   Therefore be plain in speech.

CHORUS:                            We drive out murderers.

ATHENE: And where can such a fugitive find rest and peace?

CHORUS: Only where joy and comfort are not current coin.

ATHENE: And to such end your hue and cry pursues this man?

CHORUS: Yes. He chose to become his mother's murderer.

ATHENE: Was there not some compulsive power whose
   wrath he feared?

CHORUS: And who has power to goad a man to matricide?

ATHENE: One plea is now presented; two are to be heard.

CHORUS: But he would ask no oath from us, nor swear him-
   self.

ATHENE: You seek the form of justice, more than to be just.

CHORUS: How so? Instruct me; you do not lack subtlety.

ATHENE: Injustice must not win the verdict by mere oaths.

CHORUS: Then try him fairly, and give judgement on the
   facts.

ATHENE: You grant to me final decision in this case?

CHORUS: We do; we trust your wisdom, and your father's
   name.

ATHENE: It is your turn to speak, my friend. What will you
   say?
   Your faith in justice sent you to my statue here,
   A holy suppliant, like Ixion, at my hearth;
   Therefore tell first your country, birth, and history;
   Then answer to this charge; and let your speech be plain.

ORESTES : Divine Athene, first from your last words I will
    Set one great doubt at rest. My hand is not unclean;
    I do not sit polluted at your statue's foot.
    And I will tell you weighty evidence of this.
    To a blood-guilty man the law forbids all speech,
    Till blood-drops from some suckling beast are cast on him
    By one whose office is to purge from homicide.
    Long since, these rituals were all performed for me
    In other temples; beasts were slain, pure water poured.
    That question, then, I thus dispose of. For my birth,
    I am of Argos, and you know my father well,
    For you and he joined league to make the city of Troy
    No city – Agamemnon, leader of the warlike fleet.
    When he came home, he met a shameful death, murdered
    By my black-hearted mother, who enfolded him
    In a cunning snare, which now bears witness to the stroke
    That felled my father as he cleansed the stains of war.

    When, later, after years of exile I came home,
    I killed my mother – I will not deny it – in
    Just retribution for my father, whom I loved.
    For this Apollo equally is answerable;
    He told me of the tortures that would sear my soul
    If I neglected vengeance on the murderers.
    Whether or no I acted rightly is for you
    To judge; I will accept your word, for life or death.
ATHENE : This is too grave a cause for any man to judge;
    Nor, in a case of murder, is it right that I
    Should by my judgement let the wrath of Justice loose;
    The less so, since you came after full cleansing rites
    As a pure suppliant to my temple, and since I
    And Athens grant you sanctuary and welcome you.
    But your accusers' claims are not to be dismissed;
    And, should they fail to win their case, their anger falls

Like death and terror, blight and poison, on my land.
Hence my dilemma – to accept, or banish them;
And either course is peril and perplexity.
Then, since decision falls to me, I will choose out
Jurors of homicide, for a perpetual court,
In whom I vest my judgement. Bring your evidence,
Call witnesses, whose oaths shall strengthen Justice' hand.
I'll pick my wisest citizens, and bring them here
Sworn to give sentence with integrity and truth.

*Exit* ATHENE, *to the city;* ORESTES *retires into the temple.*

CHORUS: Now true and false must change their
    names,
  Old law and justice be reversed,
  If new authority put first
  The wrongful right this murderer claims.
  His act shall now to every man
  Commend the easy path of crime;
  And parents' blood in after time
  Shall gleam on children's hands accurst,
  To pay the debt this day began.

  The Furies' watchful rage shall sleep,
  No anger hunt the guilty soul;
  Murder shall flout my lost control;
  While neighbours talk of wrongs, and weep,
  And ask how flesh can more endure,
  Or stem the swelling flood of ill,
  Or hope for better times – while still
  Each wretch commends some useless cure.

  When stunned by hard misfortune,
  On us let no man call,
  Chanting the old entreaties,
  'Come, swift, avenging Furies!

O sword of Justice, fall!'
Some parent, struck or slighted,
In loud and vain distress
Often will cry, a stranger
To the new wickedness,
Which soon shall reach and ruin
The house of Righteousness.

For fear, enforcing goodness,
Must somewhere reign enthroned,
And watch men's ways, and teach them,
Through self-inflicted sorrow,
That sin is not condoned.
What man, no longer nursing
Fear at his heart – what city,
Once fear is cast away,
Will bow the knee to Justice
As in an earlier day?

Seek neither licence, where no laws compel,
Nor slavery beneath a tyrant's rod;
Where liberty and rule are balanced well
Success will follow as the gift of God,
Though how He will direct it none can tell.
This truth is apt: the heart's impiety
Begets after its kind the hand's misdeed;
But when the heart is sound, from it proceed
Blessings long prayed for, and prosperity.

This above all I bid you: reverence
Justice' high altar; let no sight of gain
Tempt you to spurn with godless insolence
This sanctity. Cause and effect remain;
From sin flows sorrow. Then let man hold dear

His parents' life and honour, and revere
Each passing guest with welcome and defence.

Wealth and honour will attend
Love of goodness gladly held;
Virtue free and uncompelled
Fears no harsh untimely end.
But the man whose stubborn soul
Steers a rash defiant course
Flouting every law's control –
He in time will furl perforce,
Late repenting, when the blast
Shreds his sail and snaps his mast.

Helpless in the swirling sea,
Struggling hands and anguished cries
Plead with the unheeding skies;
And God smiles to note that he,
Changing folly for despair,
Boasts for fear, will not escape
Shipwreck on the stormy cape;
But, his former blessings thrown
On the reef of justice, there
Perishes unwept, unknown.

ATHENE *returns, bringing with her twelve Athenian citizens.*
APOLLO *comes from the temple, leading* ORESTES.

ATHENE: Summon the city, herald, and proclaim the cause;
Let the Tyrrhenian trumpet, filled with mortal breath,
Crack the broad heaven, and shake Athens with its voice.
And while the council-chamber fills, let citizens
And jurors all in silence recognize this court
Which I ordain today in perpetuity,
That now and always justice may be well discerned.
CHORUS: Divine Apollo, handle what belongs to you.
Tell us, what right have you to meddle in this case?

APOLLO: I came to answer that in evidence. This man
Has my protection by the law of suppliants.
I cleansed him from this murder; I am here to be
His advocate, since I am answerable for
The stroke that killed his mother. Pallas, introduce
This case, and so conduct it as your wisdom prompts.

ATHENE: The case is open. [*To the* LEADER OF THE
CHORUS] Since you are the accuser, speak.
The court must first hear a full statement of the charge.

CHORUS: Though we are many, few words will suffice. [*To*
ORESTES] And you
Answer our questions, point for point. First, did you kill
Your mother?

ORESTES:            I cannot deny it. Yes, I did.

CHORUS: Good; the first round is ours.

ORESTES:                                    It is too soon to boast:
I am not beaten.

CHORUS:            You must tell us, none the less,
How you dispatched her.

ORESTES:                        With a sword I pierced her heart.

CHORUS: On whose persuasion, whose advice?

ORESTES:                                        Apollo's. He
Is witness that his oracle commanded me.

CHORUS: The god of prophecy commanded matricide?

ORESTES: Yes; and he has not failed me from that day to this.

CHORUS: If today's vote condemns you, you will change
your words.

ORESTES: I trust him. My dead father too will send me help.

CHORUS: Yes, trust the dead now: your hand struck your
mother dead.

ORESTES: She was twice guilty, twice condemned.

CHORUS:                                        How so? Instruct
The court.

ORESTES:   She killed her husband, and my father too.

167

CHORUS: Her death absolved her; you still live.
ORESTES: But why was she
  Not punished by you while she lived?
CHORUS: The man she killed
  Was not of her own blood.
ORESTES: But I am of my mother's?
CHORUS: Vile wretch! Did she not nourish you in her own
    womb?
  Do you disown your mother's blood, which is your own?
ORESTES: Apollo, now give evidence. Make plain to me
  If I was right to kill her. That I struck the blow
  Is true, I own it. But was murder justified?
  Expound this point, and show me how to plead my cause.
APOLLO: To you, august court of Athene, I will speak
  Justly and truly, as befits a prophet-god.
  I never yet, from my oracular seat, pronounced
  For man, woman, or city any word which Zeus,
  The Olympian Father, had not formally prescribed.
  I bid you, then, mark first the force of justice here;
  But next, even more, regard my father's will. No oath
  Can have more force than Zeus, whose name has sanctioned
    it.
CHORUS: Then Zeus, you say, was author of this oracle
  You gave Orestes – that his mother's claims should count
  For nothing, till he had avenged his father's death?
APOLLO: Zeus so ordained, and Zeus was right. For their two
    deaths
  Are in no way to be compared. He was a king
  Wielding an honoured sceptre by divine command.
  A woman killed him: such death might be honourable –
  In battle, dealt by an arrow from an Amazon's bow.
  But you shall hear, Pallas and you who judge this case,
  How Clytemnestra killed her husband. When he came
  Home from the war, for the most part successful, and

Performed his ritual cleansing, she stood by his side;
The ritual ended, as he left the silver bath,
She threw on him a robe's interminable folds,
Wrapped, fettered him in an embroidered gown, and
    struck.


Such, jurors, was the grim end of this king, whose look
Was majesty, whose word commanded men and fleets.
Such was his wife who killed him – such that none of you,
Who sit to try Orestes, hears her crime unmoved.

CHORUS: Zeus rates a father's death the higher, by your
    account.
Yet Zeus, when his own father Cronos became old,
Bound him with chains. Is there not contradiction here?
Observe this, jurors, on your oath.

APOLLO:                              Execrable hags,
Outcasts of heaven! Chains may be loosed, with little harm,
And many ways to mend it. But when blood of man
Sinks in the thirsty dust, the life once lost can live
No more. For death alone my father has ordained
No healing spell; all other things his effortless
And sovereign power casts down or raises up at will.

CHORUS: You plead for his acquittal: have you asked your-
    self
How one who poured out on the ground his mother's blood
Will live henceforth in Argos, in his father's house?
Shall he at public altars share in sacrifice?
Shall holy water lave his hands at tribal feasts?

APOLLO: This too I answer; mark the truth of what I say.
The mother is not the true parent of the child
Which is called hers. She is a nurse who tends the growth
Of young seed planted by its true parent, the male.
So, if Fate spares the child, she keeps it, as one might
Keep for some friend a growing plant. And of this truth,

That father without mother may beget, we have
Present, as proof, the daughter of Olympian Zeus:
One never nursed in the dark cradle of the womb;
Yet such a being no god will beget again.


Pallas, I sent this man to supplicate your hearth;
He is but one of many gifts my providence
Will send, to make your city and your people great.
He and his city, Pallas, shall for ever be
Your faithful allies; their posterity shall hold
This pledge their dear possession for all future years.

ATHENE: Shall I now bid the jurors cast each man his vote
   According to his conscience? Are both pleas complete?

APOLLO: I have shot every shaft I had; and wait to hear
   The jurors' verdict.

ATHENE [to the CHORUS]: Will this course content you too?

CHORUS [to the jurors]: You have heard them and us. Now,
      jurors, as you cast
   Your votes, let reverence for your oath guide every heart.

ATHENE: Citizens of Athens! As you now try this first case
   Of bloodshed, hear the constitution of your court.
   From this day forward this judicial council shall
   For Aegeus' race hear every trial of homicide.
   Here shall be their perpetual seat, on Ares' Hill.
   Here, when the Amazon army came to take revenge
   On Theseus, they set up their camp, and fortified
   This place with walls and towers as a new fortress-town
   To attack the old, and sacrificed to Ares; whence
   This rock is named Areopagus. Here, day and night,
   Shall Awe, and Fear, Awe's brother, check my citizens
   From all misdoing, while they keep my laws unchanged.
   If you befoul a shining spring with an impure
   And muddy dribble, you will come in vain to drink.
   So, do not taint pure laws with new expediency.

Guard well and reverence that form of government
Which will eschew alike licence and slavery;
And from your polity do not wholly banish fear.
For what man living, freed from fear, will still be just?
Hold fast such upright fear of the law's sanctity,
And you will have a bulwark of your city's strength,
A rampart round your soil, such as no other race
Possesses between Scythia and the Peloponnese.
I here establish you a court inviolable,
Holy, and quick to anger, keeping faithful watch
That men may sleep in peace.

                          I have thus far extended
My exhortation, that Athens may remember it.
Now give your votes in uprightness, and judge this cause
With reverence for your oath. I have no more to say.

*During the following dialogue the jurors rise in turn to vote. There are two urns, one of which is 'operative', the other 'inoperative'. Each juror has two pebbles, a black and a white. Into the 'operative' urn each drops a white pebble for acquittal or a black one for condemnation; then disposes of the other pebble in the other urn, and returns to his seat.*

CHORUS: I too advise you: do not act in scorn of us,
   Your country's visitants, or you will find us harsh.

APOLLO: I bid you fear my oracle and the word of Zeus,
   And not make both unfruitful.

CHORUS [*to* APOLLO]:       Deeds of blood are not
   For your protection. Henceforth you will prophesy
   From a polluted shrine.

APOLLO:            Then what of Zeus? Did he
   Suffer pollution, when he willed to purify
   His suppliant Ixion, the first murderer?

CHORUS: You argue; but if we should fail to win this case
   We will infest the land with plagues unspeakable.

APOLLO: You have as little honour amongst elder gods
As amongst us, the younger. I shall win this case.

CHORUS: This recalls your behaviour in Admetus' house:
You bribed the Fates to let a mortal live again.

APOLLO: Was it not right to help a man who worshipped me?
Undoubtedly; besides, Admetus' need was great.

CHORUS: You mocked primeval goddesses with wine, to break
The ancient dispensation.

APOLLO:                                  Disappointment soon
Will make you vomit all your poison – harmlessly.

CHORUS: You think your youth may tread my age into the dust.
When we have heard the verdict will be soon enough
To launch my anger against Athens. I will wait.

ATHENE: My duty is to give the final vote. When yours
Are counted, mine goes to uphold Orestes' plea.
No mother gave me birth. Therefore the father's claim
And male supremacy in all things, save to give
Myself in marriage, wins my whole heart's loyalty.
Therefore a woman's death, who killed her husband, is,
I judge, outweighed in grievousness by his. And so
Orestes, if the votes are equal, wins the case.
Let those appointed bring the urns and count the votes.
                    *Two of the jurors obey her.*

ORESTES: O bright Apollo, what verdict will be revealed?

CHORUS: O Mother Night, O Darkness, look on us!

ORESTES:                                                           To me
This moment brings despair and death, or life and hope.

CHORUS: To us increase of honour, or disgrace and loss.

APOLLO: The votes are out. Count scrupulously, citizens;
Justice is holy; in your division worship her.
Loss of a single vote is loss of happiness;
And one vote gained will raise to life a fallen house.

*The votes are brought to* ATHENE. *The black and the white*
   *pebbles are even in number.* ATHENE *adds hers to the white.*
ATHENE: Orestes is acquitted of blood-guiltiness.
   The votes are even.
ORESTES:              Pallas, Saviour of my house!
   I was an exile; you have brought me home again.
   Hellas can say of me, 'He is an Argive, as
   He used to be, and holds his father's house and wealth
   By grace of Pallas and Apollo, and of Zeus
   The Saviour, the Fulfiller.' Zeus has shown respect
   For my dead father, seeing my mother's advocates,
   And has delivered me.

                    So now, before I turn
   My steps to Argos, hear the oath I make to you,
   Your country, and your people, for all future time:
   No Argive king shall ever against Attica
   Lead his embattled spears. If any man transgress
   This oath of mine, I will myself rise from the grave
   In vengeance, to perplex him with disastrous loss,
   Clogging his marches with ill omens and despair,
   Till all his soldiers curse the day they left their homes.
   But if my oath is kept, and my posterity
   Prove staunch and faithful allies to the Athenian State,
   They shall enjoy my blessing. So, Pallas, farewell;
   Farewell, citizens of Athens! May each struggle bring
   Death to your foes, to you success and victory!
                    *Exeunt* APOLLO *and* ORESTES.
CHORUS: The old is trampled by the new!
   Curse on you younger gods who override
   The ancient laws and rob me of my due!
   Now to appease the honour you reviled
   Vengeance shall fester till my full heart pours
   Over this land on every side

Anger for insult, poison for my pain –
Yes, poison from whose killing rain
A sterile blight shall creep on plant and child
And pock the earth's face with infectious sores.
Why should I weep? Hear, Justice, what I do!
Soon Athens in despair shall rue
Her rashness and her mockery.
Daughters of Night and Sorrow, come with me,
Feed on dishonour, on revenge to be!

ATHENE: Let me entreat you soften your indignant grief.
Fair trial, fair judgement, ended in an even vote,
Which brings to you neither dishonour nor defeat.
Evidence which issued clear as day from Zeus himself,
Brought by the god who bade Orestes strike the blow,
Could not but save him from all harmful consequence.
Then quench your anger; let not indignation rain
Pestilence on our soil, corroding every seed
Till the whole land is sterile desert. In return
I promise you, here in this upright land, a home,
And bright thrones in a holy cavern, where you shall
Receive for ever homage from our citizens.

CHORUS: The old is trampled by the new!
Curse on you younger gods who override
The ancient laws and rob me of my due!
Now to appease the honour you reviled
Vengeance shall fester till my full heart pours
Over this land on every side
Anger for insult, poison for my pain –
Yes, poison from whose killing rain
A sterile blight shall creep on plant and child
And pock the earth's face with infectious sores.
Why should I weep? Hear, Justice, what I do!
Soon Athens in despair shall rue
Her rashness and her mockery.

Daughters of Night and Sorrow, come with me,
Feed on dishonour, on revenge to be!

ATHENE: None has dishonoured you. Why should immortal
rage
Infect the fields of mortal men with pestilence?
You call on Justice: I rely on Zeus. What need
To reason further? I alone among the gods
Know the sealed chamber's keys where Zeus's thunderbolt
Is stored. But force is needless; let persuasion check
The fruit of foolish threats before it falls to spread
Plague and disaster. Calm this black and swelling wrath;
Honour and dignity await you: share with me
A home in Athens. You will yet applaud my words,
When Attica's wide fields bring you their firstfruit gifts,
When sacrifice for childbirth and for marriage-vows
Is made upon your altars in perpetual right.

CHORUS: O shame and grief, that such a fate
Should fall to me, whose wisdom grew
Within me when the world was new!
Must I accept, beneath the ground,
A nameless and abhorred estate?
O ancient Earth, see my disgrace!
While anguish runs through flesh and bone
My breathless rage breaks every bound.
O Night, my mother, hear me groan,
Outwitted, scorned and overthrown
By new gods from my ancient place!

ATHENE: Your greater age claims my forbearance, as it gives
Wisdom far greater than my own; though to me too
Zeus gave discernment. And I tell you this: if you
Now make some other land your home, your thoughts will
turn
With deep desire to Athens. For the coming age
Shall see her glory growing yet more glorious.

175

You, here possessing an exalted sanctuary
Beside Erechtheus' temple, shall receive from all,
Both men and women, honours which no other land
Could equal. Therefore do not cast upon my fields
Whetstones of murder, to corrupt our young men's hearts
And make them mad with passions not infused by wine;
Nor plant in them the temper of the mutinous cock,
To set within my city's walls man against man
With self-destructive boldness, kin defying kin.
Let war be with the stranger, at the stranger's gate;
There let men fall in love with glory; but at home
Let no cocks fight.

            Then, goddesses, I offer you
A home in Athens, where the gods most love to live,
Where gifts and honours shall deserve your kind good-will.
CHORUS: O shame and grief, that such a fate
    Should fall to me, whose wisdom grew
    Within me when the world was new!
    Must I accept, beneath the ground,
    A nameless and abhorred estate?
    O ancient Earth, see my disgrace!
    While anguish runs through flesh and bone
    My breathless rage breaks every bound.
    O Night, my mother, hear me groan,
    Outwitted, scorned and overthrown
    By new gods from my ancient place!
ATHENE: I will not weary in offering you friendly words.
You shall not say that you, an elder deity,
Were by a younger Power and by these citizens
Driven dishonoured, homeless, from this land. But if
Holy Persuasion bids your heart respect my words
And welcome soothing eloquence, then stay with us!
If you refuse, be sure you will have no just cause

To turn with spleen and malice on our peopled streets.
A great and lasting heritage awaits you here;
Thus honour is assured and justice satisfied.

CHORUS: What place, divine Athene, do you offer me?

ATHENE: One free from all regret. Acceptance lies with
you.

CHORUS: Say I accept it: what prerogatives are mine?

ATHENE: Such that no house can thrive without your favour
sought.

CHORUS: You promise to secure for me this place and power?

ATHENE: I will protect and prosper all who reverence you.

CHORUS: Your word is pledged for ever?

ATHENE:                                   Do I need to promise
What I will not perform?

CHORUS:                          My anger melts. Your words
Move me.

ATHENE:   In Athens you are in the midst of friends.

CHORUS: What blessings would you have me call upon this
land?

ATHENE: Such as bring victory untroubled with regret;
Blessing from earth and sea and sky; blessing that breathes
In wind and sunlight through the land; that beast and field
Enrich my people with unwearied fruitfulness,
And armies of brave sons be born to guard their peace.
Sternly weed out the impious, lest their rankness choke
The flower of goodness. I would not have just men's lives
Troubled with villainy. These blessings *you* must bring;
*I* will conduct their valiant arms to victory,
And make the name of Athens honoured through the world.

CHORUS: I will consent to share Athene's home,
    To bless this fortress of the immortal Powers
        Which mighty Zeus and Ares
        Chose for their habitation,
    The pride and glory of the gods of Greece,

177

And guardian of their altars.
This prayer I pray for Athens,
Pronounce this prophecy with kind intent:
Fortune shall load her land with healthful gifts
    From her rich earth engendered
    By the sun's burning brightness.
ATHENE: I will do my part, and win
Blessing for my city's life,
Welcoming within our walls
These implacable and great
Goddesses. Their task it is
To dispose all mortal ways.
He who wins their enmity
Lives accurst, not knowing whence
Falls the wounding lash of life.
Secret guilt his father knew
Hails him to their judgement-seat,
Where, for all his loud exclaims,
Death, his angry enemy,
Silent grinds him into dust.
CHORUS: I have yet more to promise. No ill
        wind
Shall carry blight to make your fruit-trees fade;
    No bud-destroying canker
    Shall creep across your frontiers,
Nor sterile sickness threaten your supply.
May Pan give twin lambs to your thriving ewes
    In their expected season;
    And may the earth's rich produce
Honour the generous Powers with grateful gifts.
ATHENE: Guardians of our city's wall,
Hear the blessings they will bring!
Fate's Avengers wield a power
Great alike in heaven and hell;

And their purposes on earth
They fulfil for all to see,
Giving, after their deserts,
Songs to some, to others pain
In a prospect blind with tears.

CHORUS: I pray that no untimely chance destroy
    Your young men in their pride;
And let each lovely virgin, as a bride,
    Fulfil her life with joy.
For all these gifts, you sovereign gods, we pray,
    And you, our sisters three,
    Dread Fates, whose just decree
Chooses for every man his changeless way,
You who in every household have your place,
    Whose visitations fall
    With just rebuke on all –
Hear us, most honoured of the immortal race!

ATHENE: Now, for the love that you perform
To this dear land, my heart is warm.
Holy Persuasion too I bless,
Who softly strove with harsh denial,
Till Zeus the Pleader came to trial
And crowned Persuasion with success.
Now good shall strive with good; and we
And they shall share the victory.

CHORUS: Let civil war, insatiate of ill,
    Never in Athens rage;
Let burning wrath, that murder must assuage,
    Never take arms to spill,
    In this my heritage,
The blood of man till dust has drunk its fill.
    Let all together find
      Joy in each other;
And each both love and hate with the same mind

As his blood-brother;
For this heals many hurts of humankind.

ATHENE: These gracious words and promised deeds
Adorn the path where wisdom leads.
Great gain for Athens shall arise
From these grim forms and threatening eyes.
Then worship them with friendly heart,
For theirs is friendly. Let your State
Hold justice as her chiefest prize;
And land and city shall be great
And glorious in every part.

CHORUS: City, rejoice and sing,
Who, blest and flourishing
With wealth of field and street,
Wise in your hour, and dear
To the goddess you revere,
Sit by the judgement-seat
Of heaven's all-judging king,
Who guards and governs well
Those favoured ones who dwell
Under her virgin wing.

ATHENE: We wish you joy in turn. Now I must go
And guide you to your chambers in the rock,
Lit by the holy torches
Of these who shall escort you.
With eager haste and solemn sacrifice,
Come, enter this dear earth, there to repel
Harm from our homes and borders,
And bring us wealth and glory.
Sons of the Rock of Athens, lead their way,
Welcome these Residents within your walls;
They come to bless our city:
Let our good-will reward them.

CHORUS: My blessings I repeat

On all whose homes are here,
To whom this rock is dear;
On temple and on street
Where gods and mortals meet.
And as with awe and fear
And humble hearts you greet
My presence as your guest,
So year succeeding year
Shall be more richly blest.

ATHENE: I thank you for your prayers. Now by these torches'
    gleam
I and my maidens who attend my statue here
Come to escort you to your home beneath the ground.
Young women, children, a resplendent company,
Flower of the land of Theseus, with a reverend troop
Of elder women, dressed in robes of purple dye,
Shall go with you. Honour the Friendly Goddesses;
And let the flaring lights move on, that our new guests
In coming years may grace our land with wealth and peace.

*During the last three speeches a procession has been gathering, with
    music and lighted torches, to escort the* CHORUS *from the stage;
    as they go, all sing together:*

Pass onward to your home,
Great ones, lovers of honour,
Daughters of ancient Night,
Led by the friends your peace has won;
    (And let every tongue be holy!)

On to the deep of earth,
To the immemorial cavern,
Honoured with sacrifice,
Worshipped in fear and breathless awe;
    (And let every tongue be holy!)

Come, dread and friendly Powers
Who love and guard our land;
And while devouring flame
Fills all your path with light,
Gather with gladness to your rest.
    And let every voice
Crown our song with a shout of joy!

Again let the wine be poured
By the glare of the crackling pine;
Now great, all-seeing Zeus
Guards the city of Pallas;
Thus God and Fate are reconciled.
    Then let every voice
Crown our song with a shout of joy!

# NOTES

*

## AGAMEMNON

**p. 42** *My tongue's nailed down.* The literal meaning of the Greek is 'A great ox stands on my tongue', the ox being proverbial for an immovable weight. It seems necessary to find some different but equally homely metaphor.

**p. 43** *Zeus, Pan, Apollo.* The gods care for the helpless young of animals. Cf. Calchas' address to Artemis, p. 46. The parallel between these two passages suggests that the rape of Helen and the sacrifice of Iphigenia were both abhorrent to the gods.

**p. 45** *The evil which has been.* Past evil (the killing of Iphigenia) makes them apprehensive of the future. They now proceed to tell the story of the setting-out of the expedition. The first episode, the portent of the eagles and the hare, took place as the two kings left Argos; the sacrifice of Iphigenia took place at Aulis, where they met the rest of the force.

*It was ten years ago – but I was there.* I have inserted this line to make the situation clearer. The Elders, too old to join the army, saw them off from Argos; some may even have accompanied them as far as Aulis.

*The body of a pregnant hare.* The portent's primary meaning is the destruction of Troy, with her teeming population, by Agamemnon and Menelaus. This destruction, when accomplished, will be as abhorrent to the gods as the killing of the young in the womb; therefore it behoves the Greek army to be careful to avoid all further offence, such as desecration of temples in the captured city. There is also plainly a secondary allusion to the sacrifice of Iphigenia; as the hare dies before the fulfilment of birth, so Iphigenia dies before the fulfilment of marriage. She was offered to Artemis; but 'Artemis abominates the eagles' feast.' This secondary meaning is mentioned on p. 47, 'Wreaking vengeance for a murdered child.'

**p. 46** *The army's learned Seer.* Calchas, who was with the army throughout the ten years. He prescribed human sacrifice again when Troy was captured.

P. 46 *Lovely child of Zeus.* Artemis. She and Apollo were the twin children of Leto by Zeus.

P. 47 *Who is God?* I have inserted this question here to make clear the sequence of thought; which is, that 'Let good prevail' assumes an understanding of what 'good' is; and that question leads back at once to the more fundamental problem of God, and so to the theme of this stanza. It should be noted that while Aeschylus accepts the figures of the various Olympian gods as legend and symbol, as a philosopher he asserts that God is one, and must be the author and centre of the moral universe.

P. 48 *Head-winds heavy with past ill.* The fatal head-wind at Aulis occupies a central place in the story, and supplies a recurring image throughout the trilogy.

P. 49 *Then he put on The harness of Necessity.* This is the central paradox of Fate and free-will. Both in the *Oresteia* and in other plays, notably *The Seven Against Thebes*, Aeschylus insists that though an inherited curse may make man's choice desperately hard, it is still his choice.

P. 54 *Wakeful anger of the forgotten dead.* A returning warrior (see Introduction, p. 32) must guard himself against the vengeance of the spirits of those he has killed, by undergoing a ritual purification as soon as he reaches his home. This remark of Clytemnestra's is taken by the Elders to refer to this usual precaution; but the 'forgotten dead' Clytemnestra is thinking of is Iphigenia, whom Agamemnon on his return seems indeed to have forgotten.

P. 55 *Trace that hand.* The following stanzas trace the course of Paris's sin to its final retribution.

P. 56 *Thenceforth there is no way to turn aside.* Cf. p. 50, 'Shameless self-willed infatuation Emboldens men,' etc. As in the story of Faust, there is a point beyond which the sinner cannot turn back, even though forgiveness is still offered. 'Infatuation' is in Greek *Ate*, which has been an English word, if rare, at least since Shakespeare used it of Queen Elinor in *King John*.
*In that safe dimness.* The sinner is thought of as shunning the light, lest God should find him out. Cf. *The Choephori*, p. 105,

'Yet, though the sinner cower Long years in the half-light, Or flout time's vengeance safe in total night . . .'

**p. 56** *The fiend Temptation.* The word is really 'persuasion', used here in the sense more often expressed by the English 'temptation'. But the same power which is here an agent of evil reappears in *The Eumenides* as an agent of good. See pp. 175–9.

*His fair freshness.* The allusion here is to the death of Paris, the accounts of which often mention in detail the spoiling of his effeminate beauty in the gory dust of the battlefield.

**p. 57** *Guard and groom.* The Greek word means 'chamberlains', personal servants who would be intimate with their master and mistress.

**p. 60** *An interval of some days.* I follow Professor Campbell in thinking that an interval is certainly indicated here. It is true that the action of most extant Greek plays is contained between dawn and dusk of one day; but this can hardly be maintained of the extant plays of Aeschylus, of which, besides the *Oresteia*, there are four. Of these *The Suppliants* and *Prometheus* are timeless; in *The Persians* time is irrelevant; only in *The Seven Against Thebes* is the action in any way related to the passage of a day. In the *Oresteia*, *The Eumenides* breaks the unity of place by the distance between Athens and Delphi, and the unity of time probably by several years. In *The Choephori* time is clearly limited to one day, but there are several changes of scene. So that, on the evidence of the extant work of Aeschylus, there is no reason whatever for thinking it unlikely that he should postulate an interval of anything up to fifteen days between the capture of Troy and the arrival of Agamemnon at Argos. The lines immediately preceding the interval fit the chattering dispersal of the Chorus as exactly as the following lines suit their bustling return to the stage. It is, however, possible that the Interval should come at the end of the Ode, just *before* the lines, 'Since the beacon's news was heard,' etc.

**p. 61** *You deities who watch the rising sun.* The statues of Zeus, Apollo, and Hermes stand on the eastward or south-eastward façade of the palace, facing the direction from which Agamemnon arrives.

P. 62 *Our hearts echo what you felt.* Their relief at Agamemnon's safe arrival is so deep that they could now die happy. The more sombre note of 'Our hearts were dark with trouble' naturally escapes the Herald.

P. 64 *A wife as faithful as he left.* In this and the following lines Clytemnestra uses her characteristic mixture of irony and extravagant lies, designed to baffle and disturb with innuendo.

P. 66 *Helen, the Spoiler.* The root HELE means 'destroying'. This does not mean that the name 'Helen' originally meant 'a destroyer'; but fancied derivations were a Greek pastime, and were felt to have dramatic significance.

*To hear the Zephyr breathe Gigantic . . .* The Greek says simply, 'She sailed by the breath of the giant Zephyr.' I cannot see any reason why Aeschylus should here mention that Zephyr in legend was a giant, except to suggest by the word the vast height and expanse of the sails of Paris's ship.

*Bond and pledge.* The Greek word KEDOS has two quite unrelated meanings: 'marriage-kinship' and 'grief'. A 'pledge' in marriage unites two persons and two families; but a 'bond' may be that of captivity or death.

P. 67 *The god defied.* I.e. Zeus, guardian of the laws of hospitality which Paris broke.

*A lion's cub.* The gentle young creature is a symbol of Helen as Paris and the Trojans first saw her.

P. 68 *When Earth and Time were young.* The faith expressed in this stanza gives the poet's reason for feeling that he must 'justify the ways of God to man' in the story of Agamemnon.

P. 70 *The urn of death.* Cf. the trial scene in *The Eumenides*, where a different method of voting is used. In the method Agamemnon thinks of, each judge has only one pebble, and drops it into the one urn for acquittal, or into the other for condemnation.

P. 71 *The lion rampant.* Professor Campbell has collected evidence to show that it was not unknown to have on the surface of a shield a figure of a beast which could be rotated from inside the shield as the warrior charged, thus disconcerting an enemy who was unacquainted with the device.

**P. 71** *A ranked and ravening litter.* Here is another play on words. LOCHOS means both 'newly-born young' and a 'band' of armed men; and it is here used of the Greek soldiers who emerged from the womb of the wooden horse.

*Life and long observation.* Agamemnon is ready to apply the Elders' warning in any direction but the right one.

*Where disease wants remedy . . . this body . . .* By 'this body' he means the State of Argos. The secondary application, suggested by dramatic irony, is of course to the family of Atreus and to Agamemnon's own body.

**P. 72** *Why our child is not here.* The name 'Orestes' is left till the end of the sentence, for Clytemnestra is thinking not only of him but of Iphigenia.

*Surely free from all suspicion.* Note the skill with which Clytemnestra, by refuting suspicion of Strophius (which was never entertained by anyone) precludes it from herself.

**P. 73** *The hour that slept with me.* No translation can convey the point of this line. The Greek participle meaning 'that slept with me' precedes the noun it refers to, 'hour' or 'time', which is the last word in the sentence. So that, until this last word is pronounced, dispelling all excuse for uneasiness, it seems as if the meaning were going to be, 'visions of more deaths involving you than *the man* who slept with me.'

*May Heaven's jealousy acquit us.* She means, for the ears of the Chorus, 'acquit Agamemnon and me for our abundant happiness in being reunited'; for the ears of the audience, 'acquit Aegisthus and me for the success we hope to achieve by the removal of Agamemnon.'

*For both were prolonged.* The dramatic value of this vicious snub is not merely that it still further whets Clytemnestra's appetite for revenge; but that it establishes Agamemnon as a formidable person, a worthy antagonist even for Clytemnestra.

**P. 74** *The praise of fame rings clear,* etc. A possible alternative meaning is, 'Report has other names in use For frills and fancy foot-rugs,' i.e. report calls them the follies of a braggart.

P. 74 *There is the sea.* See Introduction, p. 26.

P. 75 *Slavery is a yoke* . . . Yet Agamemnon himself has just now, by his compliance, put the yoke upon himself; as he did at Aulis, where '. . . he put on The harness of Necessity.' But Cassandra has not, like her master, learnt to bear the yoke; Clytemnestra, who can impose her will on Agamemnon, fails to gain obedience from Cassandra. 'Thus the slave proves herself superior to the conqueror, the barbarian to the Greek, the woman to the man' (R. P. Winnington-Ingram).

*Eleleleleu.* This cry is not written in the Greek MSS., but Professor Campbell includes it in his text. See Cassandra's words on p. 85, 'that cry of triumph', etc., a passage which makes it almost certain that a stage-direction indicating this cry has disappeared here.

P. 76 *Yields her kingdom in the flesh.* I.e. spirit should rule in the flesh; but flesh is now running amuck with fear, and spirit loosens the reins, knowing that the instinct of the flesh is right.

P. 81 *Prophets find bad news useful.* The Elders, really frightened by Cassandra's last utterance, find a comforting escape in this reflection.

P. 82 *Itun, Itun.* The accusative case of ITUS, which is usually spelt in English *Itys.* He was the son of Procne, whom she herself killed to punish her husband Tereus for the rape of her sister Philomela. Philomela was afterwards turned into a nightingale, and *Itun, Itun* is supposed to represent her song.

P. 83 *Cocytus, Acheron.* Two rivers of the lower world. The names mean respectively 'river of wailing' and 'river of grief'.

P. 84 *A ghastly choir.* Cassandra means the Furies, who would naturally haunt a house so steeped in crime. Aeschylus does not trouble to reconcile the older view, that the Furies punished many kinds of crime, with the later view (assumed in *The Eumenides*) that they are only concerned with the criminal who kills one of his own blood.

*The defiler of his brother's bed.* Thyestes had committed adultery with Atreus' wife Aerope.

**P. 84** *The God of Words.* A very common name for Apollo was Loxias, which is perhaps connected with LOGOS, 'a word', or perhaps with LOXOS, 'ambiguous'.

**P. 86** *She vows to drug his dram.* For this double meaning of 'a safe arrival' cf. p. 74, 'safe journey's end', and p. 91, 'thank-offering for safe journey'. A safe arrival would be celebrated both by drinking and by libation to the gods. The cup Clytemnestra is preparing for Agamemnon is his death, mingled with Cassandra's.

**P. 90** *In a silver bath.* This is certain enough; see p. 96, 'Lord of this silver-walled inheritance.'
*Zeus, lord of the lower region.* Cf. *The Choephori*, p. 117, 'Zeus of the lower earth.'

**P. 92** *Chryseis.* The daughter of a priest of Apollo in a small town near Troy, whom Agamemnon took for his concubine.

**P. 93** *Affronts both ear and heart.* This translates a single word which means 'lawlessly'; but it is used in two senses, both of which apply here: 'breaking the laws of music' and 'breaking the laws of justice'; for the word NOMOS, 'due measure', can mean both 'custom' and 'tune'.

**P. 94** *Dressed in my form, a phantom* . . . I.e. I am but an instrument of the living curse that haunts our house.

**P. 95** *His ageing days.* The word 'ageing' is not in the text; but I have felt justified in using it here, because the contrast between the immaturity of Thyestes' sons and of Iphigenia, and the maturity of Agamemnon, is more than once emphasized. See p. 94, 'A man for babes should bleed', and p. 143, 'Next in succession died a man.'

**P. 97** *A net the avenging Furies wove.* Aegisthus claims all the sanctions of justice; and with some colour. But he omits the provocation given by Thyestes to Atreus when he seduced his wife.

**P. 98** *House of Tantalus.* The Greek text says, 'House of Pleisthenes'. Pleisthenes was probably a son of Tantalus, but a link in the chain who is not often mentioned and whose name at this point merely confuses the English reader.

# THE CHOEPHORI

P. 104 *Through the hushed midnight house.* The voice was that of Cly-
temnestra, shrieking in terror at the dream which is de-
scribed on pp. 122–3.

P. 111 *Their measurements Show the same form, the same proportions.* This
statement, though it has sometimes been derided, is not so
foolish as it may seem. Professor Tucker in his edition quotes
evidence of primitive tribes even in modern times to whom
the shape of the feet is as clear a mark of family resemblance
as the face.

P. 112 *Behold the eagle's brood bereaved.* In *Agamemnon* the Atreidae
were eagles, first robbed of their young, then tearing the
pregnant hare. But Clytemnestra is also a viper in whose coils
the victim was ensnared; so Orestes too will soon (p. 123) 'be
viperous in heart and act'. In *Agamemnon* (p. 86) Clytem-
nestra was the lioness who mated with a wolf; in *Choephori*
(p. 118) 'the savage cubs the she-wolf bore Are like their
mother.'

P. 113 *With prayer and countless offerings.* This cannot but recall
Agamemnon's offering of Iphigenia; for the word used here –
not a common word – is the same as that used in *Agamemnon*,
p. 50, in the phrase, 'He endured to offer up his daughter's
life.'

*A hand so liberal.* Electra has prayed for 'clean hands and ways
unlike my mother's'. But this phrase reminds us that the
daughter of two parents both guilty of murder is now herself
planning murder.

P. 117 *Shall like to like give birth?* Cf. *Agamemnon*, p. 69, 'Like the
Powers that give it birth.'

P. 119 *His flesh was mutilated.* This probably refers to the cutting off
of hands and feet and placing them under the armpits; a
supposed precaution against the vengeance of the dead.

P. 120 *None from outside can help.* This thought is repeated on p. 133,
'Redemption from within.'

P. 123 *It was treachery they used to kill him.* Cf. *Agamemnon*, p. 95,
'The guile I used to kill him.'

**P. 125** Three examples of the lengths to which reckless passion will drive women.

*Althaea.* When her son Meleager was born she was told that he would live only until the torch that lit her palace hall was burnt out. She quickly extinguished the torch, and kept it in a safe place; but when her brothers were killed by Meleager in a fight, in her rage she lit the torch, and Meleager died.

*Scylla.* Daughter of Nisus king of Megara. When Minos besieged Megara, Scylla was bribed by him to cut off a golden hair on her father's head, on which his life depended.

*The Lemnian massacre.* All the women of Lemnos, jealous of their husbands' concubines, agreed together to kill their husbands, the concubines, and all male Lemnians. Only one woman, Hypsipyle, spared her father, Thoas.

**P. 127** *The avenging fiend.* There is a double meaning here. The fiend is the Curse or Fury that haunts the house; it waits its time and seems to have forgotten; but at last it 'pays' or 'punishes' the crime. The fiend is also Clytemnestra, whose name can be interpreted to mean 'renowned for guile', and who now 'pays' her ancient crime, i.e. suffers for it, 'in blood'.

**P. 128** *O misery! Our last defences* ... It has been argued that these lines would be more suitable in the mouth of Electra; several phrases would thus gain in point or bear a double meaning. But, apart from the fact that no MS. indicates it, a re-entry for Electra here seems to me both circumstantially improbable and dramatically confusing.

**P. 136** *Down with your sword, my son!* Clytemnestra first tries the voice of authority – when she last saw Orestes he was a little boy. Finding it has no effect, she proceeds at once to the most pathetic appeal possible; but her very words remind her of her dream.

## THE EUMENIDES

**P. 147** *Pythian.* The word is applied to Apollo, to his oracle, and to his priestess. It is derived from the Greek word meaning 'to find out by inquiry', and refers to Apollo's oracular function.

**P. 147** *Earth, Themis.* In *Prometheus* Aeschylus identifies these two – 'many names for one person' – as the mother of Prometheus. See Introduction, p. 10.

*Parnassus.* The mountain which rises close to Delphi.

*Hephaestus' sons.* Erichthonius, mythical founder of Athens, was a son of Hephaestus.

**P. 148** *People and king alike.* I.e. the Delphians and their eponymous king Delphos.

*Pallas Pronaia. Pronaia* means 'before the temple'. 'Pallas of the precincts.'

*Bromius.* Another name for Dionysus. The story of his encounter with Pentheus is told in Euripides' play *The Bacchae.*

*Fresh olive-leaves twined with white wool.* The proper equipment for a suppliant at an altar.

**P. 152** *Earth's central sacred stone.* There was in the forecourt of the Delphic temple a stone, used as an altar, and said to be the central point of the earth. It was called Omphalos, 'the navel'.

**P. 153** *Destiny.* Literally, 'the Fates'. There seems to be an allusion here to the legend that Apollo tricked the three Fates, by making them drunk, into agreeing to postpone the death of Admetus on condition that he found a willing substitute. See Euripides' *Alcestis.* The argument of the next stanza seems to be, 'Orestes shall not, like Alcestis, be rescued from death.' But the reference is somewhat faintly hinted, and to make it clear in translation would involve considerable expansion. Cf. the allusion to this story in the trial scene, p. 172.

*Some pit of punishments*, etc. Apollo abuses the Furies as being barbarous, and the barbarisms he mentions are horrors that Greeks usually associated with Oriental despotism. He means simply that the function of the Furies is 'un-Hellenic', in contrast to the Hellenic use of courts and juries.

**P. 155** *The scene changes.* Note that this change is not even covered by a choral Ode, and that the interval implied is a good deal more difficult to imagine than the time-interval in *Agamemnon.* The speech of Orestes which follows indicates that the interval may have been one of years.

192

**P. 155** *Not unclean now.* In the first scene his hands and sword were still wet with blood.

**P. 157** *She shall gain . . . myself, my country*, etc. The year before the production of this play a treaty had been made between Athens and Argos.

*At rest, at war.* The Greek says (according to the probable interpretation), 'whether standing or sitting', and refers to statues of Athene, which were made sometimes in the one posture, sometimes in the other. It was a Greek habit to refer to a statue personally, as if it were itself the deity.

*The Phlegraean plain.* This is in Chalcidice, in north-eastern Greece; it was the scene of the battle between gods and giants, in which Athene acted as general.

**P. 158** *Now, by the altar,* etc. No English version can do justice to the rhythmical force of this 'binding-spell'. A producer might well prefer to abandon the stanza printed in italics, and use the Greek. I give a transcription, with the syllables marked short and long. It would be advisable to get someone with a knowledge of Greek to suggest a reasonable pronunciation.

ĕpĭ dĕ tō tĕthŭmĕnō
tŏdĕ mĕlōs, părăkŏpā,
părăphrŏnā phrĕnŏdālēs,
hūmnŏs ēx ĕrīnŭōn,
dēsmĭōs phrĕnōn, ăphōr-
mīktŏs, aūŏnā brŏtoīs.

**P. 159** *And Hope . . . lies.* This is an attempt to render the ironic understatement of the Greek, which says, literally, 'And when he dies he is not unduly free.'

**P. 160** *Zeus, free from taint or question.* But the meaning may be rather, 'Free from taint or the duty of carrying out an enquiry.' If so, it is significant that Athene, rejecting this safeguard of divine purity, proceeds at once to institute an enquiry: 'Was there not some compulsive power . . . ? (p. 162).

*For him our dreaded footfall . . .* I.e. the punishment of abhorrent crime is a function which deeply concerns Zeus, but the exercise of it might compromise his purity; it is to relieve him that we undertake such duties.

P. 161  *Beside Scamander.* This is an allusion to a dispute between Athens and Mytilene concerning the possession of some territory near Troy, which took place about the time this play was produced.

P. 162  *But he would ask no oath.* This passage is based on the form of the preliminary enquiry which an Athenian magistrate would conduct before referring the case to the appropriate court of law. In this enquiry the plaintiff would state on oath that he had suffered injury, and the defendant that he was innocent.

P. 168  *The man she killed was not of her own blood.* This is a weak argument, for it plainly dishonours the marriage-bond. Orestes, however, instead of attacking the argument on this ground, himself makes a weak reply by asking, 'But I am of my mother's?' The obvious reply of the Chorus-leader brings the jurors' sympathy again to her side. Orestes, feeling he is out of his depth, hands over to his advocate. For the whole of this passage see Introduction, pp. 34–5.

*For man, woman, or city.* The words 'or city' will remind the audience that the influence of Delphi had tended to favour the Persians rather than to encourage Greek independence.

*Whose name has sanctioned it.* Zeus was the guardian of oaths.

P. 170  *I have shot every shaft.* Most texts attribute this speech to the Chorus and the next but one ('You have heard . . .') to Apollo. The MSS., plainly at fault, give both to the Chorus. Mr Winnington-Ingram has shown quite clearly that the arrangement adopted here is the right one.

*So, do not taint . . .* This line is not in the Greek. It is inserted to make clearer the point of the proverb about pure water, which refers to the warning phrase, 'while they keep my laws unchanged.'

P. 176  *Erechtheus.* The first king of Athens.

*To set . . . man against man.* The whole of this passage is plainly a stern warning against political disunity within Athens.

P. 181  *A resplendent company.* The Panathenaic procession. See Introduction, p. 19.

# APPENDIX

Clytemnestra's speech, 'There is the sea . . .'
(p. 74; lines 958–72 in the Oxford Text).

In the text of *Agamemnon* used for this translation, that of the late Professor A. Y. Campbell, this famous speech is transposed to come after line 929, 'Call him fortunate Whom the end of life finds harboured in tranquillity'. In the traditional text it comes after line 957, 'Treading on purple I will go into my house.' Unfortunately Professor Campbell's exposition of his reasons for this change is found only in notes still unpublished at the time of his death. I give here a provisional outline of his view (necessarily omitting numerous detailed arguments with which he supported his text), based on personal conversations with him.

The speech has two parts. In the first Clytemnestra uses two arguments to persuade Agamemnon to walk on the purple cloth: (1) We are rich and can well afford to waste our wealth; (2) I would have made such a sacrifice many times over, had an oracle prescribed it, in order to ensure your safe return. (Clytemnestra assumes that the purple cloth, after such ritual use, would not be put back into stock, but dedicated in a temple, or even destroyed – compare the ritual of breaking a wine-glass after drinking a health. The possibility of such a dedication, as the result of a vow taken in a moment of danger, is referred to again by Clytemnestra near the end of p. 74.) In the second part of the speech Clytemnestra uses obscure and figurative language to express the welcome that awaits Agamemnon when he enters his house.

If the purpose of the speech is to persuade Agamemnon to walk on the purple cloth, it should surely come at a point where he is still undecided whether he will do so or not. In the traditional text it comes immediately after he has said that he will do what Clytemnestra asks. Further, at that point he is already standing bare-footed in the chariot ready to step to the ground; and to postpone any longer the dramatic moment when his foot touches the purple seems pointless, even if (as was ingeniously done at Bradfield in 1958) Clytemnestra is made to deliver this speech standing directly in front of the chariot, so that Agamemnon cannot descend until she moves. The alternative to this, accepted by the most recent editor, is that Agamemnon should walk up the purple path to his doom while Clytemnestra makes her speech. Dramatically, this is lamentable – to us at least; and it is hard to believe that it was not so to the ancient Greeks. The significance of Agamemnon's progress to the fatal door must not be spoilt by having Clytemnestra talk all through it; and the impact of Clytemnestra's dynamic speech must not be spoilt by having Agamemnon walk all through it.

Further, this transposition seems to be suggested, if not demanded, by the movement of the plot. We know that Clytemnestra intends to kill her husband; a formidable undertaking. The tension of the drama lies in the question, Will she succeed? For success, she must have the gods on her side; Agamemnon must be persuaded to perform some act by which he will forfeit the gods' favour. When at the end of her speech Clytemnestra has the purple cloth brought in, we see her intention. When she finishes speaking, everything turns on the tone of Agamemnon's reply. That reply is so crushingly complete that her hopes of success seem shattered. What can possibly counter such a broadside of offensive rebuke? Surely not a series of lines in *stichomythia*? The line-by-line dialogue implies already a willingness to be argued with, which is certainly not there at the close of Agamemnon's speech. What produces this willingness? What but the most telling speech in the play, beginning, 'There is the sea . . .'? That is the masterpiece which produces, first, the willingness to be argued with, then its necessary result, capitulation. When we put Clytemnestra's speech here, we find that it is of almost exactly the same length as the speech to which it replies; two balanced speeches now introduce the *stichomythia* – a pattern that became familiar in Greek drama. Finally, when Agamemnon at length agrees to walk on the purple, he is now able to do so without further delay, amid the silence demanded by so defiant and irreligious an act. (See Introduction, pp. 25–7.)

If this transposition restores the true sequence, how does the speech come to be out of place in the traditional text? There exist only two MSS. which contain this portion of the play; they were both written eighteen centuries after Aeschylus. How many different copies passed on the text during those centuries? How many performances, each with its own reasons for alteration, omission, adaptation, introduced successive changes into traditional scripts? The text of this play is very much more corrupt than that of most Greek plays. Certain rules for textual conjecture can be formulated; but remembering that the MSS. are our primary evidence is not the same thing as saying that a text differing from the MSS. is necessarily improbable. Here it is best simply to state the fascinating puzzle and leave it at that.

## THE FOLLOWING BOOKS ARE SUGGESTED FOR FURTHER READING:

*Greek Tragedy*. H. D. F. Kitto
*The Greek Tragic Poets*. D. W. Lucas
*Aeschylus*. Gilbert Murray
*Aeschylus and Athens*. George Thomson
*The Harmony of Aeschylus*. E. T. Owen
*Five Stages of Greek Religion*. Gilbert Murray
*Primitive Culture in Greece*. H. J. Rose
*The Greeks*. H. D. F. Kitto
*The Greeks and their Gods*. W. K. C. Guthrie
*The Twelve Olympians*. Charles Seltman
*Form and Meaning in Drama*. H. D. F. Kitto
*The Justice of Zeus*. H. Lloyd-Jones

# THE PRONUNCIATION OF
# GREEK NAMES

W E may consider Greek names roughly in two classes.

First, those that are familiar, and have become anglicized in either the Latin form (e.g. *Delphi*, *Olympus*), or an English form (e.g. *Athens*, *Corinth*, *Priam*, *Helen*). It is felt by some to be pedantic to say *Delphoi* and *Olympos* or *Olumpos*, *Priamus* or *Priamos*, *Helena* or *Helene*. *Athenai*, *Korinthos*, seem even more strange. In some very familiar names English practice has established inconsistencies which it would be folly to interfere with; there is no reconciling *Socrates* with *Aristotle* on any principle; nor will anyone recognize *Platon*.

Secondly, there are the less familiar and the entirely unfamiliar names, which we transliterate into English with the change of the Greek U into English Y, the Greek K into English C in certain positions, the Greek final -AI and -OI into Latin -AE and -I, while leaving the singular endings in -OS unchanged instead of substituting the Latin -US. To this class belong *Mycenae*, *Delos*, possibly *Makistos*; but not *Euripus* or *Asopus*; while *Arachnaios* or *Arachnaeus* will probably alternate according to the taste of the speaker.

For the forms I have used in this translation I claim neither consistency nor even final correctness, for in some instances there may be no 'correct' form; but I hope to have avoided evident incorrectness.

## Diphthongs

EU as in English *deuce*. Note that names ending in *-eus* rhyme with *deuce*. The pronunciation *ee-us* is incorrect (even though Shakespeare insists on it for *Aegeus* in *A Midsummer Night's Dream*).

AU as in English *fraud*; but some names, e.g. *Menelaus*, have the *a* and *u* separate, with accent on the *a*, *ay-us*.

OE and AE to be pronounced *ee*, e.g. *Phoebus*.

OU to be pronounced *oo*, e.g. *Ouranos*.

## Consonants

C should be hard, except before *e* and *i*.

CH should be hard as in *loch*.

G should be hard as in *gate*, except in words which have become thoroughly anglicized, e.g. *Aegean*.

S should be as in *this*, not as in *these*.

Final E is always pronounced.

The following list is intended to include all proper names used in this book about which there could be any reasonable doubt. The sign ′ indicates accent.

Achae′an. First *a* short.

A′cheron. Both *a* and *e* short.

Achi′lles. *a* short.

Aege′an. The *g* usually soft.

Aegeus. The *g* usually soft.

Ae′gipla′nctus.

Aegi′sthus.

A′ërope. *e* and *o* both short.

Agame′mnon. Both *a*'s short.

Althae′a.

Apo′llo. *a* short.

Aphrodi′te. *i* long as in *die*.

Arachnae′us.

Areo′pagus. All the vowels short.

Ares. *a* as in *hare*.

A′rtemis. *e* short.

Aso′pus. *o* long as in *hope*.

A′tre-id. *a* long as in *hate*.

A′treus. The *a* is strictly short as in *hat*, but is more usually pronounced long as in *hate*.

Ca′lchas.

Cho-e′phori. *e* long as in *these*, *i* usually pronounced like a long *e*, according to the alternative spelling *Choephoroe*.

Chry′se-is. *y* long as in *dye*; but *y* short as in *mythical* is a common pronunciation.

Cili′ssa.

Cithae′ron. *i* short.

Clytemne'stra. *y* long as in *dye*. (This name has been irrevocably and incorrectly anglicized.)

Cocy'tus. *o* long as in *coke*, *y* as in *dye*.

Cory'cian. *o* short, *y* short as in *mythical*.

Cro'nos. Both *o*'s short as in *on*.

De'lphi. *i* either as in *die*, or like English final -*y*.

Ephia'ltes. First *e* short.

Ere'chtheus. Both *e*'s short.

Erichtho'nius. All the vowels short.

E'ris. *e* short.

Euboe'a.

Eume'nides. *e* short in second syllable.

Euri'pus. *i* as in *die*.

Ge'ryon. *e* short as in *very*.

Gorgo'pis. *o* as in *hope*.

Hephae'stus. *e* long like EE.

He'ra. *e* as in *here*.

Hypsipyle. *i* short, both *y*'s as in *mythical*.

I'da. *i* as in *hide*.

I'lion. *i* as in *pile*.

I'nachus. *i* as in *fine*, *a* short.

Iphigeni'a. *e* short; first *i* long as in *ripe*, but often pronounced short.

Itu'n. *i* short, *u* long, somewhere between *tune* and *boon*.

Ixi'on. First *i* short, second *i* as in *lion*.

Le'da. *e* like *ee*.

Lo'xias. *o* as in *box*.

Ly'cian. *y* as in *mythical*.

Mai'a. *ai* like *i* in *messiah*.

Maki'stos. *a* short.

Menela'us. Both *e*'s short, *a* as in *lay*.

Messa'pian. *a* as in *say*.

Mi'nos. *i* as in *mine* (always thus incorrectly anglicized).

Ody'sseus. *y* as in *mythical*.

Orestei'a. *ei* variously pronounced as *e* in *panacea* or *i* in *messiah*.

Ou'ranos. *a* short.

Pe'leus. *e* long like EE.

Pe'lops. *e* short as in *tell*.

Phi′neus. *i* long as in *fine*.

Pho′cis. *o* long; *c* usually soft, as in *Phocian*, but sometimes pronounced hard.

Phoe′bus.

Plei′stos. *ei* like *y* in *ply*.

Posei′don. First *o* short, *ei* like *i* in *side*.

Pri′am. To rhyme with *I am*.

Prome′theus. *o* short, *e* like *ee*.

Py′lades. *y* as in *dye*, *a* short.

Py′thian. *y* short as in *mythical*.

Sa′lamis. Both *a*'s short.

Scama′nder. Both *a*'s short.

Scy′lla. *y* short as in *mythical*, *c* usually silent.

Si′mo-is or Simo′is. Both *i*'s short.

So′lon. First *o* long.

Stro′phius. *o* short.

Stry′mon. *y* long as in *dye*.

Ta′ntalus. Both *a*'s short.

The′mis. *e* short as in *stem*.

The′seus. *e* long as in *these*.

The′tis. *e* short as in *set*.

Thy-e′stes. *y* long as in *dye*, *e* short as in *best*.

Ti′tan. *i* long as in *tight*.

Trito′nian. *i* long as in *trite*.

Ty′ndareos. *y* short as in *mythical*, *a* short, *e* short, *o* short as in *loss*.

# THE HOUSE OF ATREUS

*

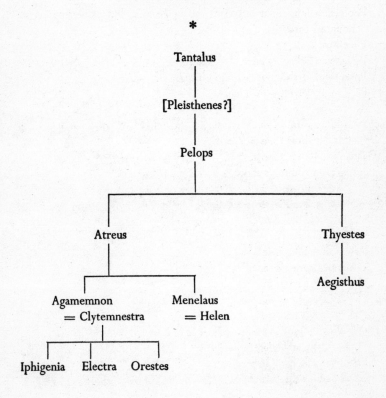

# PENGUIN ONLINE